FIRST AID

FIRST ON THE SCENE

ACTIVITY BOOK

FIRST EDITION 1994

St. John Ambulance

First Edition - 1994
First Impression 1994 - 145,000
Second Impression 1995 - 145,000
Third Impression 1996 - 50,000
Fourth Impression 1997 - 75,000
Fifth Impression 1997 - 75,000
Sixth Impression 1998 - 100,000
Seventh Impression 1999 - 75,000
Eighth Impression 2000 - 100,000
Ninth Impression 2000 - 100,000

St. John Ambulance
312 Laurier Avenue East
Ottawa, Ontario
K1N 6P6

Canadian Cataloguing in Publication Data

Main entry under title:

    First aid : first on the scene : standard level : activity book

Includes index
ISBN 0-929006-63-1

    1. First aid in illness and injury.   2. CPR (First aid).   3. First aid in illness and injury—Problems, exercises, etc.   4. CPR (First aid)—Problems, exercises, etc. I. St. John Ambulance.

RC86.8.F576   1994   616.02'52   C94-900907-5

EpiPen® Auto Injector is a registered trademark of the EM Industries, Inc.
Ana-Kit® is a registered trademark of Miles Allergy Products Ltd.
Tylenol® is a registered trademark of McNeil Consumer Products.
Tempra® is a registered trademark of Mead Johnson Canada.

Cover design: Beth Haliburton
Cover photograph: Richard Desmarais
Cover art direction: David Craib
Illustrations: Stanley Berneche

Printed in Canada
Stock No. 6500

CONTENTS

STUDENT INFORMATION

St. John Ambulance Emergency and Standard Level first aid courses are nationally standardized programmes. They are based on performance objectives and well defined training standards which are contained in the Instructor's Guide for these courses.

This **self-instruction activity book** is part of a sequenced training programme, consisting of videos, instructor-led practical and activity book exercises.

Certification requirements

The training standards specify the minimum requirements for certification. Courses may be expanded, if necessary, to include additional material required to meet local needs.

To receive a certificate in *First Aid–Standard or Emergency Level,* you must obtain:

▶ a satisfactory pass on the practical exercises, and

▶ a minimum mark of 70% on each section of the written examination

Your first aid certificate is valid for three years from the month the course was successfully completed.

Note: First aid skills, and CPR skills in particular, deteriorate very quickly unless they are practised regularly. Recertification every three years in first aid and annual retraining in CPR is recommended.

The Manual

First on the Scene, The Complete Guide to First Aid and CPR, first edition, is the reference manual for this course. You may use the manual:

▶ as supplementary reading during the course, if time permits, or

▶ as reference material after the course

USE OF THE ACTIVITY BOOK

Before starting your activity book exercises, you should have completed the Course Registration Form contained at the back of this activity book and have handed it to your instructor.

Welcome to the activity book exercises.

This self-instruction book will help you to learn the first aid theory for the *First Aid–Standard or Emergency Level* course and will prepare you for the final written examination. Your instructor will tell you which exercises to complete and when to do them.

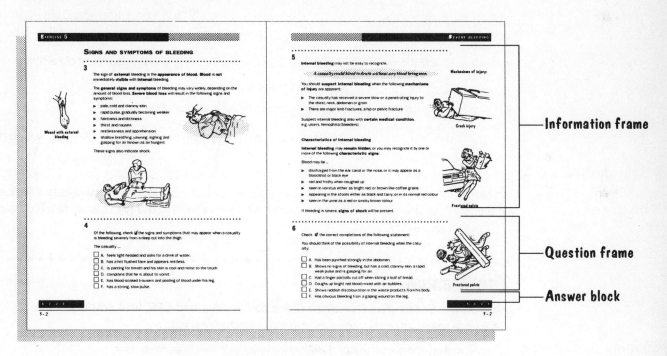

Each exercise consists of **teaching units** called **frames.**

Each frame is numbered and contains either:

▶ **information** for you to read, or

▶ **questions** for you to answer

The **correct answer** to each question appears in the **answer block** located at the bottom of the page.

How to do the activity book exercises

. . . .

1. Tear off the **cursor** attached to the back cover.

2. Use the cursor to cover the answer block until you have marked your answers to the question.

3. To **check** your answers, **slide the cursor to the side** as far as the end of the answer block. This will **reveal the correct** answer(s) in the answer block.

4. If your answer is wrong, read the question again, draw a line through your wrong answer and write in the correct one.

5. If you do not know the answer to a question, look at the answer frame, mark the correct answer in the appropriate space and read the question again.

There are several types of questions used in this activity book to reinforce your learning. Four examples are given below:

. . . .

Multiple choice type:

Check ☑ the correct completion to the statement below.

The aim of first aid for a minor, open wound is to:

☐ A. Prevent itching.

☐ B. Send the casualty to medical help.

☐ C. Control bleeding and prevent infection.

☐ D. Check the area around the wound.

Note: Multiple choice questions may have more than one right answer.

C

True or false type:

Mark each of the following statements as true **(T)** or false **(F)**:

☐ A. Spurting blood is more difficult to stop than flowing blood.
☐ B. Bleeding always looks the same, no matter where it comes from.

A.T   B.F

Order type:

Number the following first aid actions in the order you should perform them:

☐ A. Send for medical help.
☐ B. Assess responsiveness.

A.2   B.1

Match type:

Match each situation with the appropriate safety measure.

Situations

☐ A. A girl gulps down a soft drink while chewing on her hamburger.

☐ B. A man eats a sandwich while trying to steer his car.

Safety measures

1. Avoid other activities when you are eating.

2. Don't eat and drink at the same time.

A.2   B.1

Instructor-led exercises:

The Instructor-led exercises will give you the opportunity to discuss and develop key ideas with the help of your instructor. To fill in the blanks properly, your instructor will give you the appropriate information. Should you do your activity book exercises at home, the answers to the instructor-led exercises are contained in Addendum B.

Instructor-led Exercise

A. Good air exchange	**B. Poor air exchange**	**C. No air exchange**
A1. The person _____ speak.	B1. The person _____ speak.	C1. The person _____ speak.
A2. The facial colour is _____.	B2. The facial colour is _____.	C2. The facial colour is _____.
A1. can	B1. cannot	C1. cannot
A2. reddish	B2. bluish	C2. bluish

EMERGENCY SCENE MANAGEMENT

Introduction to first aid

1

What is first aid?

First aid is the emergency help given to an injured or suddenly ill person using readily available materials.

The objectives of first aid are to:

▶ preserve life

▶ prevent the injury or illness from becoming worse

▶ promote recovery

Who is a first aider?

A first aider is someone who takes charge of an emergency scene and gives first aid.

First aid symbol

First aider arriving at the scene with a first aid kit

2

Mark each of the following statements as true **(T)** or false **(F)**.

☑T A. First aid is the immediate help you give to a person who is hurt or feels sick.

☑F B. You should never use anything except special dressings and bandages made for first aid.

☑T C. You may keep someone alive by giving first aid.

☑T D. Wounds have a better chance of healing if you give prompt and appropriate first aid.

☑F E. A first aider is a person who stops at a car crash and looks at the scene.

A.T B.F C.T D.T E.F

3

What can you do as a first aider?

You can help a person in need. The principles of the **Good Samaritan Laws** will protect you, as long as you:

▶ **act in good faith** and volunteer your help

▶ **tell the person you are a first aider**

▶ **get permission** (consent) to give first aid before touching the casualty. Use your common sense and consider the age and the condition of the casualty

▶ **ask** the parents or guardian for permission if the person is an infant or young child

▶ **have implied consent**. If the person does not **respond** to you, you can give first aid. Implied consent exists because the casualty is unconscious and does not object to your help

▶ **use reasonable skill and care** according to your level of training. Give the care you would like to get if you were in the casualty's position

▶ **do not abandon (leave) the person** once your offer of help has been accepted

Can I help?

Identify yourself as a first aider

4

While walking in the park, you come across an elderly woman who has slipped on the ice. She is moaning in pain. What should you do? Check ☑ all correct answers below.

☑ A. Stop and see if you can help the person to feel better.

☑ B. You offer to help because you believe in good deeds.

☐ C. Immediately examine the person for any injuries.

☑ D. Introduce yourself as first aider and ask her to allow you to help.

☑ E. Give first aid to the best of your knowledge and ability.

☐ F. As soon as you have calmed down the lady, leave her alone.

5

What is medical help?

Medical help is the treatment given by, or under the supervision of, a medical doctor at an emergency scene, while transporting a casualty, or at a medical facility.

Doctor arriving on scene

What is a casualty?

A person who is injured or who suddenly becomes ill is called a casualty.

Age guidelines for a casualty

For first aid and CPR techniques, a casualty is considered to be:

◆   **an adult** – eight years of age and over
◆   **a child** – from one to eight years of age
◆   **an infant** – under one year of age

Ambulance arriving

Adult

Child

Infant

Use these guidelines with **common sense** in choosing the appropriate first aid and CPR techniques. Consider the size of each casualty when making your decision.

Casualty with first aider

6

Mark each of the following statements as true **(T)** or false **(F)**.

▢   A.   First aid is considered "medical help", if you have taken a first aid course.
▢   B.   An ambulance attendant gives "medical help" because he works under the supervision of a doctor.
▢   C.   A choking person who is unable to breathe is called a casualty.
▢   D.   The term infant describes a baby who is less than one year old.
▢   E.   A very small, delicate nine year-old should be treated as an adult when you give first aid.

A.F B.T C.T D.T E.F

Universal precautions in first aid

7

Some people are afraid to give first aid. They think they might catch a disease from the casualty. The risk of a serious infection being transmitted when giving first aid is small. Use the following **universal precautions** to minimize this risk and give first aid safely.

▶ **Wash your hands** with soap and running water immediately after any contact with a casualty

▶ **Wear vinyl or latex gloves** whenever you might be in touch with the casualty's blood, body fluids, open wounds or sores

▶ **Handle** sharp objects with extra care

▶ **Minimize** mouth-to-mouth contact during artificial respiration by using **a mask** or **a face shield** designed to prevent disease transmission

A face mask or face shield should:

▶ have a **one-way valve**

▶ be **disposable** or have a disposable valve

▶ be stored in an **easily accessible** place

Follow the manufacturer's instructions on how to use, care for and dispose of a mask and shield properly.

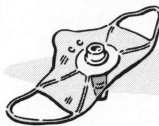

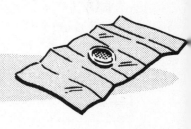

8

Which of the following actions should you take to protect yourself from infection when giving first aid? Check ☑ your choice of answers.

☑ A. Avoid touching or being splashed by a casualty's blood or body fluids.

☑ B. Place an effective barrier between you and the casualty's body fluids.

☐ C. Don't give help to people you don't know.

☑ D. Keep from pricking yourself when touching needles or other sharp things.

☑ E. Be prepared with a first aid kit that includes disposable gloves and a face mask/shield.

How to remove gloves

. . . .

9

Gloves that have been used are contaminated and may spread infection. Take them off without touching the outside. Follow the steps below:

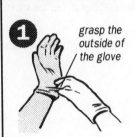

① *grasp the outside of the glove*

Grasp the cuff of one glove.

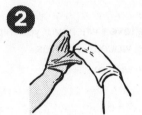

②

Pull the cuff towards the fingers, turning the glove inside out.

③

As the glove comes off, hold it in the palm of your other hand.

④ ⚠ *do not touch the outside of the glove*

Slide your fingers under the cuff of the other glove.

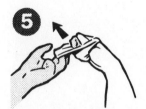

⑤

Pull the cuff towards the fingers over the first glove.

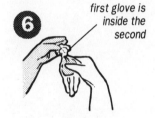

⑥ *first glove is inside the second*

Tie a knot in the top of the outer glove and dispose of properly— see below.

⑦

Wash hands with soap and running water as soon as possible.

Torn gloves
. . . .

If you tear your gloves while giving first aid, take them off right away. Wash your hands if possible, and put on a new pair of gloves.

Proper disposal
. . . .

Seal the used gloves in a plastic bag and put them in your household garbage.

Check with your instructor for specific regulations in your area.

Principles of emergency scene management (ESM)

. . . .

10

Scene survey

Emergency scene management (ESM) is the sequence of actions you should follow at the scene of an emergency to ensure that safe and appropriate first aid is given.

The order of the steps in ESM, including the priorities of first aid, may change, depending on the circumstances.

The **ESM** has four steps, usually in this order:

Primary survey

▶ scene survey

▶ primary survey

▶ secondary survey (taught as an elective lesson). This step may not need to be done if first aid for life-threatening conditions has been given and medical help is on the way.

▶ ongoing casualty care until hand over

Secondary survey

Emergency scene

. . . .

11

Ongoing casualty care

Of the following sentences, check ☑ the correct statements regarding emergency scene management.

☐ A. You should perform emergency scene management in the same order no matter what the type of injury or illness is.

☑ B. Emergency scene management starts with the survey of the scene and ends when you have handed over the casualty to medical help.

☐ C. You have to do all four steps of emergency scene management every time you give first aid.

☑ D. Following the steps of emergency scene management will help you to give the best possible care to a casualty.

12

Scene survey

The order of steps in the scene survey may change, but in most cases, you will do them in this order:

▶ take charge of the situation. If head/spinal injuries are suspected, tell casualty not to move.

▶ call for help to attract bystanders

▶ assess hazards at the scene and make the area safe for yourself and others

▶ determine the number of casualties, what happened and the mechanism of injury for each

▶ identify yourself as a first aider. Offer to help and obtain consent.

▶ if head/spinal injuries are suspected, do not move the casualty. Provide and maintain manual support for the head and neck.

▶ assess the casualty's responsiveness. If the casualty is not responsive, send or go for medical help.

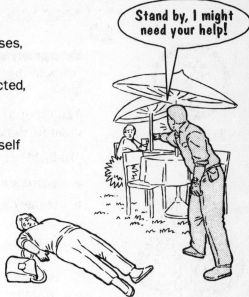

Scene survey

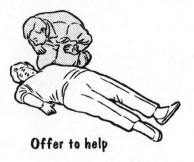

Offer to help

Assess responsiveness

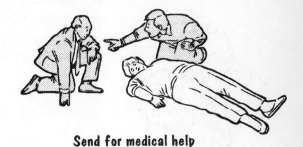

Send for medical help

13

Mark each of the following statements as true **(T)** or false **(F)**.

A. When approaching an emergency scene, the first thing you should do is take the lead and try to get someone to help.

B. At a car crash site, you give first aid without worrying about further dangers to yourself and the casualty.

C. To give appropriate first aid, you should check how many people are hurt and how badly.

D. Before you touch an injured person, you should introduce yourself and ask if you can help.

E. If you think that a casualty's neck has been hurt, tell him not to move. Steady his head and neck with your hands or show a bystander how to do this.

A.T B.F C.T D.T E.T

14

To help you to decide on the urgency of getting medical help, find out about the . . .

Scene survey

Number of casualties

▶ How many people were hurt

Casualty crumpled at the bottom of stairs

History (what, how, why)

▶ The full story of what happened

▶ How the injuries or illness happened

▶ The circumstances leading to or surrounding the incident

Body hits steering wheel

Mechanism of injury

▶ The force that causes the injury and the way it is applied to the body

Important information when you are assessing the mechanism of injury includes:

▶ the type of force

▶ the height of a fall

▶ the speed of a vehicle involved

▶ the location on the body

The greater the force, height or speed, the more likely it is that injuries will be life-threatening.

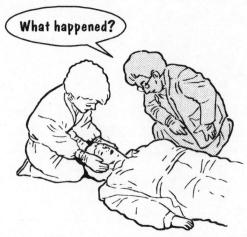

What happened?

Worker falling off ladder

15

Place a check mark ☑ beside the described mechanisms of injury that are more likely to cause life-threatening injuries and would require fast medical help.

☑ A. A high speed car crash involving several people.

☐ B. Bumping into someone on the sidewalk.

☑ C. A person diving into a shallow pool and hitting his head.

☐ D. A heavy box falling on a person's foot.

☑ E. A truck crushing somebody against a wall.

☑ F. A person falling off the roof of a house.

16

To help you decide what first aid to give to a casualty, you should find out as much as possible about the casualty's injury or illness. You need three kinds of information:

▶ history
▶ signs and
▶ symptoms

History

▶ **Ask** the conscious casualty "what happened?"
▶ **Ask** bystanders "what happened?"
▶ **Observe** the scene

Signs

Signs are conditions of the casualty **you can see, hear, feel or smell.**

▶ **Observe** the casualty
▶ **Examine** for indications of injury or illness

Symptoms

Symptoms are **things the casualty feels** and may be able to describe.

▶ **Ask** the conscious casualty how she feels
▶ **Listen** to what the casualty says

17

Identify the information of each statement below as either history, sign or symptom by writing the appropriate number into the boxes provided.

History **1**   Sign **2**   Symptom **3**

3 A. A casualty tells you he feels cold.
2 B. There is blood soaking through the shirt on a casualty's arm.
2 C. A casualty's skin is cold and clammy to the touch.
1 D. A man tells you that he slipped on a patch of ice.
3 E. A young boy says he feels sick.
1 F. You see an empty bottle of sleeping pills near an unconscious person.

A.3 B.2 C.2 D.1 E3 F.1

Primary survey

18

The primary survey is the first step in assessing the casualty for life-threatening conditions and giving life-saving first aid.

In the primary survey you check for the **priorities of first aid**. These are:

A. Airway – to ensure a clear airway

B. Breathing – to ensure effective breathing

C. Circulation – to ensure effective circulation

Even if there is more than one casualty, you should perform a primary survey on each casualty in turn. Give life-saving first aid only.

19

From the following statements, check ☑ all correct endings to the following two statements.

The purpose of the primary survey is to:

☐ A. Find all injuries.

☑ B. Find the conditions posing an immediate danger to life.

☐ C. Give complete treatment to all injuries.

Immediate threats to life include the following conditions:

☑ D. A blocked airway.

☑ E. Severe bleeding inside the body.

☐ F. A broken arm.

☑ G. Stopped breathing.

Steps of the primary survey

. . . .

20

The sequential steps of the primary survey should be performed in **the position found**, unless it is impossible to do so.

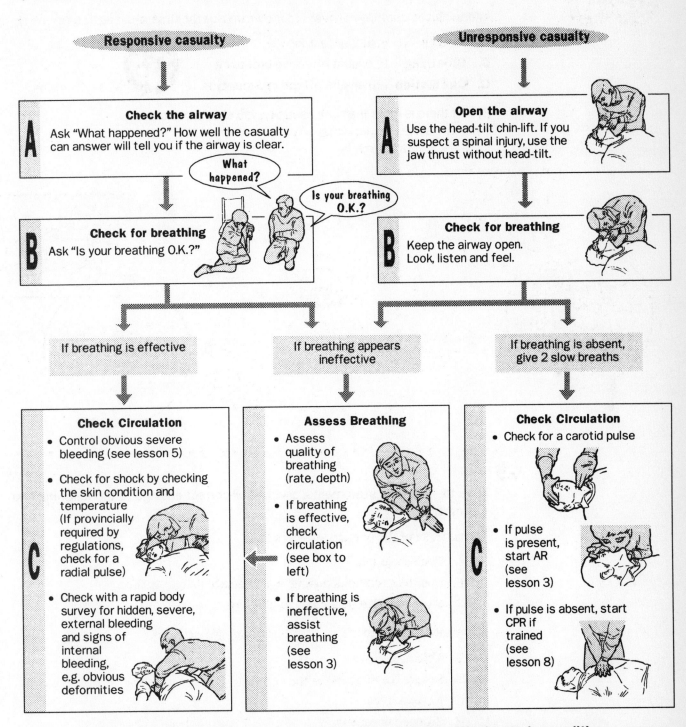

Responsive casualty

Unresponsive casualty

A **Check the airway**
Ask "What happened?" How well the casualty can answer will tell you if the airway is clear.

What happened?

Is your breathing O.K.?

A **Open the airway**
Use the head-tilt chin-lift. If you suspect a spinal injury, use the jaw thrust without head-tilt.

B **Check for breathing**
Ask "Is your breathing O.K.?"

B **Check for breathing**
Keep the airway open.
Look, listen and feel.

If breathing is effective

If breathing appears ineffective

If breathing is absent, give 2 slow breaths

Check Circulation
- Control obvious severe bleeding (see lesson 5)
- Check for shock by checking the skin condition and temperature (If provincially required by regulations, check for a radial pulse)
- Check with a rapid body survey for hidden, severe, external bleeding and signs of internal bleeding, e.g. obvious deformities

C

Assess Breathing
- Assess quality of breathing (rate, depth)
- If breathing is effective, check circulation (see box to left)
- If breathing is ineffective, assist breathing (see lesson 3)

Check Circulation
- Check for a carotid pulse
- If pulse is present, start AR (see lesson 3)
- If pulse is absent, start CPR if trained (see lesson 8)

C

When you check the ABC's, give first aid as soon as you find any life-threatening condition.
If you find any deformities, manually steady and support the injured part until medical help takes over.

21

You have finished the scene survey. The mechanism of injury does not lead you to suspect a spinal injury. You know that the casualty is unresponsive. This means you have consent to help. You have to do the primary survey to find out if the casualty has any life-threatening injuries.

Keeping the priorities of first aid in mind, place these first aid actions in the **right sequence**. Write the appropriate number into the boxes provided.

A. Check breathing.

B. Check how the skin feels. Is it dry, wet, cool, warm?

C. Open the airway.

D. Check quickly if the casualty has other life-threatening injuries.

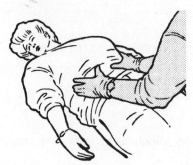

Ongoing casualty care until hand over

22

Following immediate first aid, you must **maintain the casualty in the best possible condition until hand over to medical help**.

▶ Instruct a bystander to maintain manual support of head and neck, if head/spinal injuries are suspected

▶ Continue to steady and support any injuries manually, if needed

▶ Give first aid for shock

- reassure the casualty often
- loosen tight clothing
- place the casualty in the best position for her injury or illness
- cover the casualty to preserve body heat

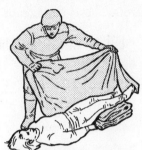

Shock position

▶ Monitor the casualty's condition (ABC's) and note any changes

▶ Give nothing by mouth

▶ Record the casualty's condition, any changes that may occur and the first aid given

▶ Protect the casualty's personal belongings

▶ Do not leave the casualty until medical help takes over

▶ Hand over to medical help and report on the incident, the casualty's condition and the first aid given

Supporting head and neck   **Recovery position**

23

An ambulance is expected soon.

Which of the actions listed below should you take to care for a conscious casualty following immediate first aid? Check off ☑ your choices.

☑ A. Place a blanket under and over the casualty to maintain body temperature.

☑ B. Check skin temperature and condition frequently.

☑ C. Provide hand support to injured body parts.

☐ D. Leave the casualty alone without further checking.

☑ E. Report to medical personnel on the casualty's condition and the help given.

☑ F. Make sure that the casualty doesn't lose any valuables.

A B C E F

Objectives

••

Following the videos and upon completion of your practical skills and this activity book exercise, in an emergency situation, you will be able to:

▶ apply the knowledge of terms used in first aid

▶ apply the knowledge of legal implications when giving first aid

▶ apply the principles of safety when giving first aid

▶ apply the principles of first aid

▶ apply the principles of emergency scene management

▶ perform a scene survey

▶ perform a primary survey

▶ perform ongoing casualty care until hand over

▶ perform the sequential steps of emergency scene management

For further information on emergency scene management, please refer to:
First on the Scene, the St. John Ambulance first aid and CPR manual, chapter 1, available through your instructor or any major bookstore in your area.

EXERCISE 2

SHOCK, UNCONSCIOUSNESS AND FAINTING

1

Shock is a condition of **inadequate circulation** to the body tissues. It results when the brain and other vital organs are deprived of oxygen. The development of shock can **be gradual or rapid.**

Shock may be present with most injuries and illnesses.

Shock can be life threatening and needs to be recognized and cared for immediately.

Common causes of severe shock	
Cause of shock	**How it affects the circulation**
▶ breathing problems (ineffective or absent breathing)	not enough oxygen in the blood to supply the vital organs
▶ severe bleeding, external or internal, including major fractures	not enough blood in circulation to supply all vital organs
▶ severe burns	loss of fluids, reducing amount of blood to fill the blood vessels
▶ spinal cord injuries	nervous system can't control the size of blood vessels and blood pools away from vital organs
▶ heart attack	heart is not strong enough to pump blood properly
▶ medical emergencies, e.g. diabetes, allergies, poisoning	these conditions may affect breathing, heart and nerve function

2

Of the following sentences, check ☑ each true statement.

☑ A. Shock occurs when vital body parts do not receive enough blood.

☑ B. A casualty with severe bleeding will show signs of shock.

☐ C. Shock is caused only by life-threatening injuries.

☐ D. A casualty always shows signs of shock right after the injury occurs.

☑ E. Shock may become life-threatening.

Signs and symptoms of shock

3

The **signs** and **symptoms** of shock may not be obvious immediately, but any of the following may appear as shock progresses.

You may see:

- ▶ restlessness
- ▶ decreased consciousness
- ▶ pale skin at first, later bluish grey
- ▶ bluish/purple colour to lips, tongue, earlobes and fingernails*
- ▶ cold, clammy skin
- ▶ profuse sweating
- ▶ vomiting
- ▶ shallow, irregular breathing; could be rapid and gasping for air
- ▶ a weak, rapid pulse (in later stages the radial pulse may be absent)

* **Note:** If the casualty has dark skin, the inside of the lips, the mouth, the tongue and the nail beds will be blue; the skin around the nose and mouth greyish.

The casualty may tell you of:

- ▶ feelings of anxiety and doom
- ▶ being confused and dizzy
- ▶ extreme thirst
- ▶ nausea
- ▶ faintness
- ▶ pain

Check skin condition

4

From the choices below, check ☑ the correct completion for the following statement. Write the appropriate choice number into the boxes provided:

	When a casualty is in shock, usually the ...	Choice 1	Choice 2
1	A. skin is	white	reddish
2	B. skin is	dry	moist
2	C. skin is	warm	cold
1	D. breathing is	fast	slow
1	E. pulse is	fast	slow
2	F. casualty feels	calm	uneasy
1	G. casualty feels	thirsty	hungry

A.1 B.2 C.2 D.1 E.1 F.2 G.1

First aid for shock

- -

5

To prevent shock from becoming worse:

► **give prompt and effective first aid for any injury or illness**

► reassure the casualty often

► loosen tight clothing at neck, chest and waist

► place the casualty into the best position for the condition

► cover the casualty to preserve body heat

► place a blanket under the casualty, if available. Ensure movement does not aggravate injuries

► give nothing by mouth

► moisten lips only if the casualty complains of thirst

► monitor the casualty's condition (ABC's) and note any changes

► continue ongoing casualty care until hand over to medical help

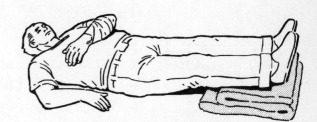

**Shock position
feet and legs raised
about 30 cm (12 inches)
Conscious casualty**

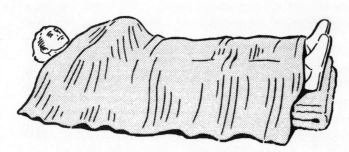

Covered casualty in shock position

- -

6

A conscious casualty is bleeding from a large slash on his forearm. His skin is cold and moist. His lips and earlobes appear bluish. Of the following, check ☑ the first aid actions you should take to prevent the casualty's condition from becoming worse.

☑ A. Give immediate first aid for the wound.

☐ B. Place the casualty into the recovery position.

☑ C. Place covers under and over the casualty to keep him warm.

☐ D. Give the casualty water to drink since he is complaining of severe thirst.

☐ E. Rub the casualty's limbs vigorously to improve his circulation.

☑ F. Avoid causing the casualty more discomfort.

Positioning of a casualty in shock

7

The **position** you use for a casualty **depends on the casualty's condition.** Always consider the casualty's comfort when choosing a position.

▶ To prevent further injury, support a casualty with suspected head/spinal injuries in the:

Position found

▶ To ease breathing, place a casualty with breathing difficulty, e.g. heart attack, asthma, into the:

Semisitting position

▶ To maintain an open airway, place the unresponsive casualty into the:

Recovery position

▶ To increase blood flow to the vital organs, place the conscious casualty into the:

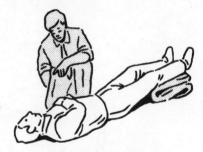

Shock position

8

Match the condition of each casualty with the position you would use to prevent shock and aggravation of injury. Place the appropriate number in the boxes provided.

Condition	Position
3 A. Possible neck injury.	1. Recovery position
1 B. Unresponsive but breathing.	2. Semisitting position
4 C. A conscious casualty's leg is bleeding severely.	3. Position found
2 D. Breathing difficulty due to chest pain.	4. Shock position

A.3 B.1 C.4 D.2

First aid for shock—review

· ·

9

The following question is based on the video, your practical exercise and this activity book exercise.

Your friend is working alone in a wood workshop. The chain saw slips and causes a large slash in your friend's lower arm. The cut is bleeding profusely and your friend is pale and sweating as you arrive.

What sequence of actions would you follow at this emergency scene to give appropriate first aid and slow down the progress of shock?

[2] A. Check the airway by asking: "Where do you hurt?"

[4] B. Expose the wound and control severe bleeding.

[1] C. Survey the scene.

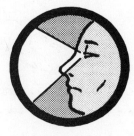

[3] D. Check breathing by asking: "Is your breathing O.K.?"

[6] E. Give ongoing casualty care.

[5] F. Check the skin condition and temperature; and perform a rapid body survey.

A.2 B.4 C.1 D.3 E.6 F.5

Unconsciousness

10

When you assess a casualty and find her unresponsive, you should immediately:

▶ send, or go for medical help

If the casualty remains unresponsive, she is considered to be unconscious.

Unconsciousness indicates a serious medical situation. Many injuries and illnesses are complicated by the loss of consciousness, e.g. head injuries, breathing emergencies, heart attack, poisoning, shock and fainting.

Unconsciousness is a _breathing emergency_.

If the unconscious casualty is lying on his back, the airway may become blocked by the tongue falling to the back of the throat, or by fluids draining into the airway. Maintaining effective breathing is the _first priority_.

▶ Look, listen and feel to determine if the casualty is breathing

▶ **Recheck breathing** frequently

▶ If the casualty stops breathing, give artificial respiration immediately.

First aid for an _unconscious_ casualty (when medical help is on the way)

▶ Perform a primary survey

▶ Give first aid for any life-threatening conditions

▶ Loosen restrictive clothing

▶ Place the casualty into the recovery position, if injuries permit

▶ Give ongoing casualty care until hand over to medical help

Any change in the casualty's condition should be observed and noted, and described to medical personnel when the casualty is handed over.

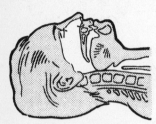

Tongue blocking the airway

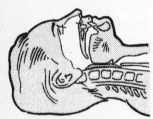

Fluids blocking the airway

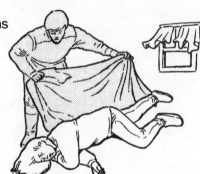

Recovery position

11

A woman collapses in the shopping mall. When you call out to her and tap her on the shoulders, you determine that she is unresponsive (unconscious). Order the following actions according to your priorities by placing the appropriate number into the squares provided:

1️⃣ A. Ask a bystander to telephone for an ambulance.

3️⃣ B. Apply first aid for life-threatening conditions.

4️⃣ C. Loosen the casualty's collar and belt.

2️⃣ D. Perform a primary survey.

5️⃣ E. Place the casualty in the recovery position, if injuries permit.

A.1 B.3 C.4 D.2 E.5

Fainting

. . . .

12

Fainting is a brief loss of consciousness caused by a **temporary shortage of oxygen to the brain.**

Fainting may be caused by:

▶ fatigue, hunger or lack of fresh air

▶ fear and anxiety

▶ long periods of standing or sitting

▶ severe pain, injury or illness

The following may warn you that a person is about to faint:

▶ you may observe paleness and sweating

▶ the casualty may complain of feeling sick and dizzy

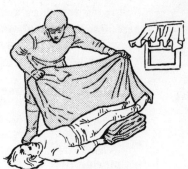

Shock position

 First aid for the person who feels faint

 First aid for the person who has fainted

Act quickly (you may be able to prevent her from fainting):

▶ lay the person down with legs raised about 30 cm (12 in) (shock position)

▶ ensure a supply of fresh air

▶ loosen tight clothing around the neck, chest and waist

If you cannot lay the person down:

▶ have the person sit with the head and shoulders lowered

A person who has fainted is temporarily unconscious. The first aid is the same as for the person who is unconscious (see opposite page).

When the casualty regains consciousness:

▶ make her comfortable

▶ keep her lying down for 10 to 15 minutes

Sitting position

. . . .

13

When a person in a small, overcrowded meeting room turns pale, and says that she feels sick and unsteady, what should you do? Check ☑ the correct answers.

☑ A. Open the windows or door.

☐ B. Tilt her head back and press a cold towel on her forehead.

☑ C. Unbutton her shirt at the neck and loosen her belt.

☑ D. Place her at rest on the back and put a rolled-up jacket under her ankles.

☐ E. Obtain medical help immediately.

A   C   D

Objectives

∙ ∙

Following the video and upon completion of your practical skills and this activity book exercise, in an emergency situation, you will be able to:

▶ **recognize shock**

▶ **provide first aid for shock**

▶ **recognize unconsciousness**

▶ **provide first aid for unconsciousness**

▶ **recognize fainting**

▶ **provide first aid for fainting**

For further information on first aid for shock, unconsciousness and fainting, please refer to: *First on the Scene*, the St. John Ambulance first aid and CPR manual, chapter 1, available through your instructor or any major bookstore in your area.

ARTIFICIAL RESPIRATION–ADULT

10 min

Introduction to breathing emergencies

1

We must breathe to live!

Breathing is the movement of air in and out of the lungs.

Air is taken in and out of the lungs by **the respiratory system** which has three main parts:

► the airway
► the lungs and
► the diaphragm

Air reaches our lungs through the **airway**.

Respiration is the process of exchange of oxygen (O_2) and carbon dioxide (CO_2) in the body.

► The air we breathe in contains **oxygen,** which is important to life
► The air we breathe out contains **carbon dioxide**, a waste product of the body

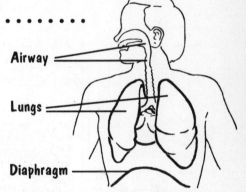

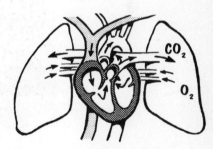

Gas Exchange

2

Check ☑ the correct statements below:

☑ A. The airway is the passage through which air flows to get from the nose and mouth to the lungs.

☑ B. The function of breathing allows air to pass in and out of the lungs.

☐ C. Carbon dioxide is the most important part of the air we breathe in.

☑ D. Our bodies need a frequent new supply of oxygen to survive.

A   B   D

Causes of breathing emergencies

3

The causes of breathing emergencies can be classified into **three major groups:**

▶ there is not enough oxygen in the air

▶ the heart and lungs are not working properly

▶ the airway is blocked—the person is choking

Life-threatening breathing emergencies can result from:

▶ suffocation   ▶ heart attack

▶ airway obstruction   ▶ near-drowning

▶ head/spinal injuries   ▶ open chest wound

▶ electric shock   ▶ poisoning

▶ drug overdose   ▶ allergic reactions, e.g. asthma

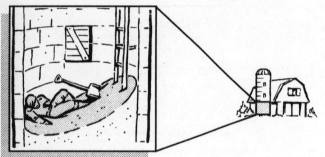

4

Check ☑ the correct completions to the following statements. Breathing emergencies occur when:

A. a person is deprived of ...

   ☐ 1. carbon dioxide in inhaled air.

   ☑ 2. oxygen in inhaled air.

B. air is not reaching a person's lungs because of a blocked ...

   ☐ 1. nasal passage.

   ☑ 2. airway.

C. a person has poor functioning of the ...

   ☑ 1. respiratory system.

   ☐ 2. muscles in the body.

Signs of breathing emergencies

5

When breathing **stops** or is **ineffective**, the body is deprived of oxygen. This is called a breathing emergency.

After **4 minutes** without oxygen, brain damage may result.

You must act immediately to restore breathing or assist breathing!

Be alert for signs of breathing emergencies:

Breathing has **stopped**, when . . .

► the chest does not rise and fall

► air movement cannot be heard or felt

Ineffective breathing is generally characterized by . . .

► very slow and shallow breaths, 10 or less per minute

► very fast and shallow breaths, about 30 or more per minute

► laboured and noisy breathing, gasping for air

► sweaty skin

► fatigue

► a bluish colour to the skin

► decreased level of consciousness

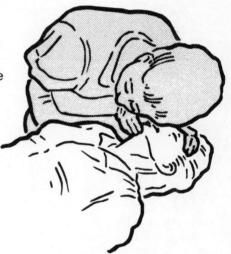

Check for breathing

6

From the following statements, check ☑ the signs which may indicate a breathing emergency:

☐ A. The chest expands and relaxes with ease.

☑ B. Rapid, irregular chest movement.

☑ C. No chest movement when you watch for breathing.

☐ D. Regular and quiet breaths.

☑ E. A casualty's lips and earlobes show blue discolouration.

☑ F. A great effort needed to breathe, making the casualty very tired.

B C E F

Effective breathing

7

Effective breathing usually is . . .

◆ without pain or effort
◆ easy and quiet
◆ with even steady rhythm

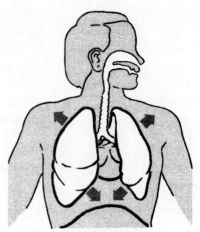

**Breathing in—
lungs inflate**

To check the **effectiveness** of the casualty's breathing, you assess the . . .

◆ breathing rate
◆ breathing depth and quality
◆ skin colour

Breathing rate

◆ Is the number of breaths in one minute
◆ The average breathing rate for a healthy adult at rest is in the range of **10 to 20 breaths per minute**

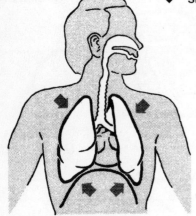

**Breathing out—
lungs deflate**

8

Mark each statement below as true (**T**) or false (**F**):

A. A person having 14 breaths a minute fits within the normal range of breathing.

B. Breathing in and breathing out should be smooth and painless.

C. A casualty's breathing is adequate, when you observe deep, sucking breaths.

D. If you suspect that a casualty's breathing is ineffective, count the number of breaths per minute and check the skin colour.

E. You should immediately try to breathe for a person who shows no signs of air moving in or out of the lungs.

A.T B.T C.F D.T E.T

First aid for breathing emergencies

9

When breathing stops, a person requires **immediate first aid**.

▶ You must get oxygen into the casualty's lungs

▶ The oxygen content of the air you breathe out is **enough to sustain** the life of a non-breathing person
The best way to do this is by blowing into the casualty's mouth. This is called **mouth-to-mouth artificial respiration (AR)**

Mouth-to-mouth AR

Blowing into the casualty's nose is another method of AR, the **mouth-to-nose method of AR**.

▶ Use the mouth-to-nose method when . . .

■ the mouth cannot be opened

■ the casualty has injuries about the mouth or jaw

■ your mouth cannot fully cover the casualty's mouth

**Mouth-to-nose AR
with shield**

**Mouth-to-mouth AR
with shield**

10

From the listing below, check☑ the correct statements relating to first aid for a non-breathing casualty.

☑ A. You can keep a person alive by blowing into her mouth or nose.

☑ B. The mouth-to-mouth method of AR is the best way you can get air into the casualty's lungs.

☐ C. If a casualty has a broken chin, use the mouth-to-mouth method of AR.

☑ D. For a casualty who has wounds around the lips, your choice of AR should be the mouth-to-nose method.

Mouth-to-nose method of AR

. . . .

11

The basic techniques for the mouth-to-nose method are the same as for the mouth-to-mouth, **except that you breathe through the casualty's nose.**

The mouth-to-mouth method is modified for the mouth-to-nose method by the following techniques:

Mouth-to-nose

- ▶ **tilt** the head back using the head-tilt chin-lift
- ▶ **close** the casualty's mouth with your thumb
- ▶ **cover** the casualty's nose with your mouth to give ventilations
- ▶ **give a ventilation and watch** the chest rise
- ▶ **open** the casualty's mouth between breaths and remove your mouth from the casualty's nose to let the air out
- ▶ **look, listen** and **feel** for air movement

. . . .

12

Check ☑ the correct completions for the following statement. When using the mouth-to-nose method of artificial respiration, you ...

A. blow air into the casualty's ...

- ☐ 1. mouth.
- ☑ 2. nose.

B. prevent air leakage by using your thumb to close the ...

- ☑ 1. mouth.
- ☐ 2. nose.

C. allow air to escape between breaths by opening the ...

- ☑ 1. mouth.
- ☐ 2. nose.

Assisted breathing

13

You may have to assist a casualty to breathe if he has severe breathing difficulties.

The **responsive** casualty may resist your efforts to assist breathing.

▶ **Reassure** the casualty and **explain** what you are trying to do and why it is needed

▶ Do not attempt to assist breathing if the casualty remains uncooperative

The **unresponsive** casualty with ineffective breathing ...

▶ is in urgent need of your assistance

Mouth-to-mouth with shield (head-tilt chin-lift)

How to provide assisted breathing

The technique for assisted breathing is the same as for mouth-to-mouth AR, except for the timing of the ventilations.

If the breathing rate is below 10 breaths per minute ...

▶ match the casualty's inhalations. Give additional ventilations between the casualty's own breaths to a combined total of 1 breath every 5 seconds

If the breathing rate is greater than 30 breaths per minute ...

▶ assist every second breath to slow the casualty's breathing rate. This will result in more effective breathing

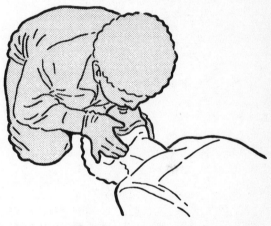

Mouth-to-mouth with face mask (jaw-thrust)

14

From the options below, check ☑ the correct completion to the following statement:

You should provide assisted breathing, for severe respiratory distress, when the casualty is:

☑ A. Breathing less than 10 times per minute.

☐ B. Conscious and refusing your help to assist him in his breathing.

☑ C. Breathing 35 times per minute.

☐ D. Unconscious, breathing quietly and has a good skin colour.

A C

Gastric distension and vomiting during AR

15

Gastric distension and **vomiting** during AR are usually caused by **increased air in the stomach**. This happens when . . .

▶ the airway is not completely open

▶ ventilations are given too quickly and with too much force causing air to enter the stomach. This prevents effective ventilation

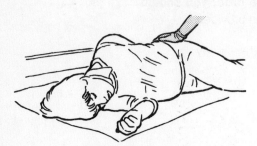

Gastric distension

To reduce the risk of gastric distension:

▶ ensure an open airway

▶ give slow breaths

▶ use only enough air to make the chest rise

Vomiting

If vomiting occurs during AR:

▶ turn the casualty to the side with her head turned down

▶ wipe the mouth clear of vomitus

▶ reposition the casualty on her back

▶ reassess breathing and pulse

▶ resume ventilations

16

Check ☑ the correct procedures that should be followed . . .

A. to lessen the possibility of air getting into the casualty's stomach:

☑ 1. recheck and maintain an open airway.

☑ 2. avoid breathing too fast and too strongly into the casualty.

B. when vomiting occurs:

☑ 1. position the casualty for good drainage. Clear her mouth, check breathing and pulse and continue AR.

☐ 2. rinse the casualty's mouth thoroughly after clearing.

A.1 A.2 B.1

Artificial respiration—review

• •

17

The following questions are based on the videos, your practical exercises and this activity book exercise.

You witness a near-drowning on a beach with a few bystanders standing around the casualty. It wasn't a diving incident and there is no indication of head/spinal injuries. You take charge and begin emergency scene management.

Number the following first aid actions for this casualty **in the order you should perform them.** Place the appropriate numbers in the squares provided.

6 A. Check for a carotid pulse.

3 B. Open the airway.

1 C. Assess responsiveness.

5 D. Give two slow breaths.

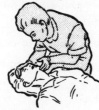

7 E. Continue giving one breath every five seconds.

4 F. Check for breathing.

2 G. Send a bystander to get medical help.

Get medical help!

Objectives

· ·

Following the video and upon completion of your practical skills and this activity book exercise, in an emergency situation, you will be able to:

◆ apply the basic knowledge of the respiratory system

◆ recognize breathing emergencies

◆ perform mouth-to-mouth artificial respiration (AR) on an adult casualty

◆ perform mouth-to-mouth AR on an adult casualty with suspected head/spinal injuries

◆ perform mouth-to-nose AR on an adult casualty

◆ deal with two complications that may occur when giving AR

◆ provide assisted breathing

For further information on first aid for breathing emergencies, please refer to: *First on the Scene*, the St. John Ambulance first aid and CPR manual, chapter 4, available through your instructor or any major bookstore in your area.

CHOKING–ADULT

10 min

uses– Steak, liquor,
children– Hot Dogs, Popcorn, Peanuts, Peanut Butter / Balloons

Signs of choking and first aid

1

A person chokes when the airway is partly or completely blocked and airflow is reduced or cut off. A choking person may die if first aid is not given **immediately**.

A person's airway can be either: **partially** or **completely** blocked.

A **partially** blocked airway results in either:

▶ **good air exchange**

▶ **poor air exchange**

With a **completely** blocked airway, there is:

▶ **no air exchange**

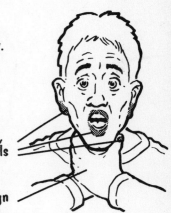

discolouration of lips, earlobes and fingernails

universal sign of choking

2 Instructor-led Exercise 4

A. Good air exchange	B. Poor air exchange	C. No air exchange
A1. The person _____ speak.	B1. The person _CANNOT_ speak.	C1. The person _CANNOT_ speak.
A2. Coughing and gagging are _____.	B2. Coughing and gagging are _weak + ineffective_.	C2. Coughing and gagging are _____.
A3. You may hear _____ when trying to breathe.	B3. You may hear _____ when trying to breathe.	C3. There will be _____; the person _____ breathe.
A4. The facial colour is _DARKER_	B4. The facial colour is _BLUE / GREY_	C4. The facial colour is _Blue / GREY_
A5. Stand by and _____.	B5. Start _FIRST AID_ for choking.	C5. Start _____ for choking.

Answers: Addendum A

4 - 1

Causes and prevention of choking

· ·

3

Choking is a life-threatening **breathing emergency**. A choking person may die if first aid for choking is not given **immediately.**

Common causes of choking are:

▶   food or some other object stuck in the throat

▶   the tongue of an unconscious person falling to the back of the throat

▶   blood or vomit collects in the throat

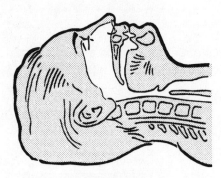
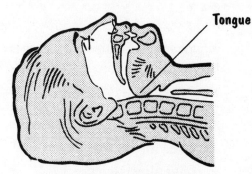

Tongue

Clear airway   **Blocked airway by tongue**

· ·

4

Check ☑ the correct answers from either choice 1 or choice 2 to complete the following statements.

Choice 1   Choice 2

When a casualty is choking and has poor or no air exchange . . .

☐ A. the air passages are clear.   ☐ A. the air passages are blocked.

☐ B. there is little or no air   ☐ B. air flows freely into and out
          getting to the lungs.   of the lungs.

☐ C. his life is in danger.   ☐ C. his life is not in danger.

When a casualty is unconscious . . .

☐ D. his air passages open   ☐ D. his tongue may block the air
          wider.   passages.

A.2 B.1 C.1 D.2

5

Choking may be caused by:

- ► trying to swallow large pieces of food
- ► eating and drinking while doing something else
- ► drinking too much alcohol before or during a meal
- ► gulping drinks with food in your mouth

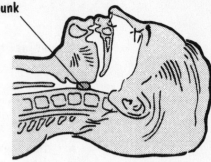

Food chunk

Airway blocked by food chunk

Avoid choking by taking these precautions:

- ► chew food well before swallowing
- ► avoid talking and laughing while chewing food
- ► drink alcohol in moderation before and during meals
- ► avoid other physical activities while eating

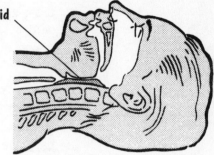

Liquid

Airway partially blocked by liquid

6

Listed below are dangerous situations that could cause choking.

Match each situation with the appropriate safety measure. Place the correct number in the boxes provided.

Situations	Safety measures
☐ A. A teenager shoves a hot dog into his mouth and gulps it down quickly.	1. Don't eat and drink at the same time.
☐ B. A man eats a sandwich while driving his car.	2. Cut food into small pieces and chew it well before you swallow.
☐ C. A girl gulps down a soft drink while chewing on her hamburger.	3. Avoid other activities when you are eating.
	4. Cut food lengthwise so it won't get caught in the throat.

A.2 B.3 C.1

Self-administered first aid for choking

7

Abdominal thrusts

When you are alone and choke and **you cannot speak, breathe or cough,** you can help yourself.

▶ Try to call for medical help (call 911 if available in your area) or to attract attention

Using your hands:

▶ place a fist above your navel

▶ grasp the fist with the other hand

▶ press inward and upward forcefully. Make each thrust distinct, with the intent to dislodge the obstruction

▶ repeat thrusts until the obstruction is relieved

Using furniture:

▶ position your abdominal area, slightly above the hips, along the counter, table edge or the back of a chair

▶ press forcefully into the edge to apply pressure. Make each thrust distinct, with the intent to dislodge the obstruction.

▶ repeat thrusts until the obstruction is relieved

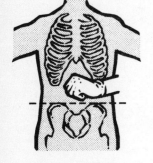

Abdominal thrusts

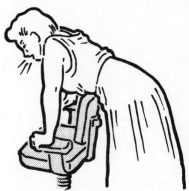

8

You are alone, eating your dinner. You suddenly find yourself choking on a piece of meat. From the following actions, check ☑ the procedures that could help you to cough up the piece of food.

- ☐ A. Drink a glass of water to wash down the food.
- ☐ B. Give yourself repeated, strong abdominal thrusts with your fist.
- ☐ C. Dial 911 immediately for medical help, if you can.
- ☐ D. Bend over the edge of your dining table and push sharply against your abdomen.
- ☐ E. Push your back several times against the wall.

9

Chest thrusts

When you are in the **late stages of pregnancy** or if you are **very obese,** abdominal thrusts cannot be applied effectively.

▶ Try to call for medical help or to attract attention

The following procedure creates a pressure similar to a chest thrust performed by a first aider:

▶ make a fist and place it thumb side down in the middle of your chest
▶ with your head turned to the side, fall against a wall hard enough to produce a chest thrust
▶ make each thrust distinct, with the intent to clear the obstruction
▶ repeat this procedure until the obstruction is relieved

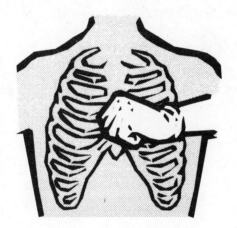

Chest thrusts

10

When you give first aid for choking, which of the following persons would require chest thrusts?

Check ☑ your choices.

☐ A. An average sized woman who is unconscious.
☐ B. A young man who is extremely overweight.
☐ C. A young woman in her last month of pregnancy.
☐ D. A very tall and muscular athlete.

First aid for choking—review

11

The following questions are based on the videos, your practical exercises and this activity book exercise.

A choking person clutches her throat, is red in the face and is coughing forcefully and loudly.

From the first aid procedures shown below, check ☑ the appropriate action you should take.

☐ A. Landmark for abdominal thrusts.

☐ B. Stand by and encourage coughing.

☐ C. Give up to five chest thrusts.

☐ D. Give up to five abdominal thrusts.

12

A choking person is conscious and has great difficulty breathing. Her lips are bluish and she is unable to answer your question, "Are you choking?"

From the first aid procedures shown below, check ☑ the one action you should take immediately.

☐ A. Use a hooked finger sweep in the casualty's mouth to remove the obstruction.

☐ B. Send for medical help immediately.

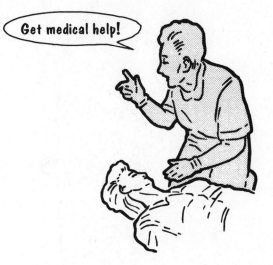

Get medical help!

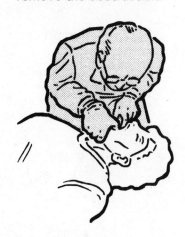

☐ C. Encourage the casualty to cough up the obstruction.

☐ D. Give abdominal thrusts until the obstruction is relieved or the person becomes unconscious.

D

13

A conscious choking casualty becomes unconscious. Number the first aid actions for this casualty **in the order you should do them**. Place the appropriate number in the boxes provided.

☐ A. Try to ventilate, reposition the head and try again.

☐ B. Ease her to the floor and call or go for medical help.

☐ C. Landmark and give abdominal thrusts.

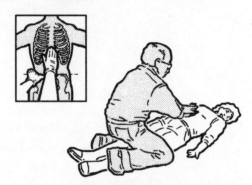

☐ D. Open the airway.

☐ E. Open the mouth using the tongue-jaw lift.

☐ F. Finger-sweep the mouth.

Ongoing casualty care until hand over

14

When a choking person's airway has been cleared and ...

▶ the casualty **remains conscious:**

- monitor breathing and circulation frequently
- stay with the casualty until breathing is well established and skin colour has returned to normal
- urge the casualty to see a medical doctor

▶ the casualty **regains consciousness:**

- monitor breathing and circulation frequently
- give first aid for shock
- stay with the casualty until medical help takes over
- urge the casualty to see a medical doctor

▶ the casualty **remains unconscious:**

- monitor breathing and circulation frequently and assist breathing if necessary
- place the casualty into the recovery position
- give first aid for shock
- stay with the casualty until medical help takes over

Note: Choking manoeuvres can cause internal damage.

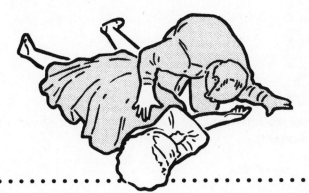

15

Check ☑ the correct completions to the following statement. When an airway obstruction has been removed by abdominal or chest thrusts, and normal breathing has been restored, the casualty should:

- ☐ A. Require no medical help.
- ☐ B. Be observed closely to ensure complete recovery.
- ☐ C. Be placed into the recovery position if not fully conscious.
- ☐ D. Be seen by a doctor to check for possible injuries.

B C D

Objectives

· ·

Following the videos and upon completion of your practical skills and this activity book exercise, in an emergency situation you will be able to:

▶ take measures to prevent choking

▶ recognize choking

▶ provide first aid for a choking adult

▶ provide ongoing casualty care until hand over for a casualty whose airway has been cleared

For further information on first aid for choking, please refer to:
First on the Scene, the St. John Ambulance first aid and CPR manual, chapter 3, available through your instructor or any major bookstore in your area.

SEVERE BLEEDING

Wounds

1

A **wound is any break in** the continuity of **the soft tissues** of the body.

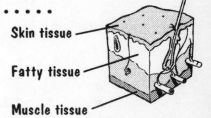

Skin tissue

Fatty tissue

Muscle tissue

A wound usually **results in bleeding.** Depending on the location of the wound, it may be either . . .

▶ **external bleeding:** blood escapes from the surface wound and can be seen, or

▶ **internal bleeding:** blood escapes from tissues inside the body and cannot be seen directly

Depending on the blood vessels that are damaged, bleeding can be either:

▶ **arterial bleeding:** blood is bright red and spurts with each heart beat from the damaged artery. Arterial bleeding is serious and often hard to control.

▶ **venous bleeding:** blood is dark red and flows steadily. It will stop more readily when being controlled.

Break in the continuity of the soft tissues

2

Mark each of the following statements as either true (**T**) or false (**F**):

☑ A. Loss of blood usually occurs when there is a break in the skin.

☑ B. A deep cut on a finger is an example of a wound with internal bleeding.

☑ C. When there are injuries inside the body, blood will leak into the surrounding areas.

☑ D. Spurting blood is more difficult to stop than flowing blood.

☑ E. Bleeding always looks the same, no matter where it comes from.

Arterial bleeding

Venous bleeding

A.T B.F C.T D.T E.F

Signs and symptoms of bleeding

3

The sign of **external** bleeding is the **appearance of blood. Blood** is **not** immediately **visible** with **internal** bleeding.

General signs and symptoms of bleeding may vary widely, depending on the amount of blood loss. **Severe blood loss** will result in the following signs and symptoms:

► pale, cold and clammy skin

► rapid pulse, gradually becoming weaker

► faintness and dizziness

► thirst and nausea

► restlessness and apprehension

► shallow breathing, yawning, sighing and gasping for air (known as air hunger)

These signs also indicate shock.

Wound with external bleeding

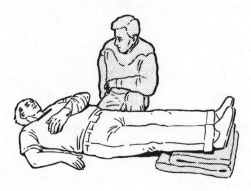

4

Of the following, check ☑ the signs and symptoms that may appear when a casualty is bleeding severely from a deep cut into the thigh.

The casualty . . .

☑ A. feels light-headed and asks for a drink of water.

☐ B. has a hot flushed face and appears restless.

☑ C. is panting for breath and his skin is cool and moist to the touch.

☑ D. complains that he is about to vomit.

☑ E. has blood-soaked trousers and pooling of blood under his leg.

☐ F. has a strong, slow pulse.

A C D E

5

Internal bleeding may not be easy to recognize.

A casualty can bleed to death without any blood being seen.

You should **suspect internal bleeding** when the following **mechanisms of injury** are apparent:

▶ the casualty has received a severe blow or a penetrating injury to the chest, neck, abdomen or groin

▶ there are major limb fractures or a hip or pelvic fracture

Suspect internal bleeding also with **certain medical conditions**, e.g. ulcers, hemophilia (bleeders).

Mechanisms of injury:

Crush injury

Characteristics of internal bleeding

Internal bleeding may **remain hidden**, or you may recognize it by one or more of the following **characteristic signs**:

Blood may be . . .

▶ discharged from the ear canal, the nose, or it may appear as a bloodshot or black eye

▶ red and frothy when coughed up

▶ seen in vomitus either as bright red, or brown like coffee grains

▶ appearing in the stools either as black and tarry, or in its normal red colour

▶ seen in the urine as a red or smoky brown colour

If bleeding is severe, **signs of shock** will be present.

Fractured pelvis

6

Check ☑ the correct completions of the following statement:

You should suspect internal bleeding when the casualty:

☑ A. Has been punched hard in the stomach.

☑ B. Shows no signs of external bleeding, but has a cold, clammy skin, a rapid, weak pulse and is gasping for air.

☐ C. Had a finger partially cut off when slicing a loaf of bread.

☑ D. Coughs up bright red blood mixed with air bubbles.

☑ E. Shows reddish discolouration in the waste products from his body.

☐ F. Has obvious bleeding from a gaping wound on the leg.

Fractured upper leg (femur)

A B D E

First aid principles for severe external bleeding

Direct pressure

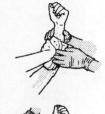

Elevation

7

Severe bleeding is an immediate threat to life.
You must act quickly!
If bleeding remains uncontrolled, shock and death may result

Control severe bleeding by:

▶ **direct pressure** to the bleeding site

- Apply continuous pressure with your hand over a pad of dressings, or with the casualty's bare hand. You may have to bring the edges of the wound together before applying pressure if the wound is large and gaping
- Continue pressure by securing dressings with a firm bandage
- If dressings become blood soaked, do not remove them. Apply additional dressings and secure with fresh bandages

▶ **elevation**

- If injuries permit, raise an injured limb above the level of the heart. This will help reduce blood flow to the wound
- Elevate an injured limb as much as the injury and the casualty's comfort will permit

▶ **rest**

- Place the casualty at rest. The preferred position is lying with lower legs raised about 30 cm (12 inches) if injuries permit

Steady and **support** the injured part and give ongoing casualty care while awaiting medical help.

8

Your co-worker has cut his forearm on a sharp knife and blood is flowing freely from the wound.

Of the following actions, check ☑ the correct procedures you should take to control the bleeding.

- ☑ A. Tell the casualty to press firmly on the wound, raise his arm and lay him down, then go for the first aid kit.
- ☑ B. Place several layers of dressings on the wound and maintain pressure.
- ☐ C. Replace all wet dressings with dry ones.
- ☐ D. Lower the casualty's arm below heart level after you have applied the bandage.
- ☑ E. Provide support for the injured arm and continue to monitor the casualty's condition.

Rest

Impaired circulation

9

Some injuries and first aid procedures may result in reduced blood flow to the limbs:

▶ **injuries at, or close to, a joint** may pinch an artery

▶ **a bandage** that is too tight

▶ **injury to a major blood vessel**

Checking temperature before bandaging

To check for impaired circulation below the injury:

▶ **compare** the **temperature** and **colour** of the injured limb below the injury (fingers or toes) to the uninjured limb before and after bandaging

  ▪ any drop in temperature in the limb is probably caused by a reduced blood flow

Checking temperature after bandaging

▶ **perform a nailbed test**

  ▪ press on a fingernail or toenail until it turns white

  ▪ release pressure; note how long it takes for the normal colour to return

  ▪ if it returns quickly, blood flow is good

  ▪ if it remains white or regains colour slowly, blood flow is impaired

To improve impaired circulation caused by too tight bandages, you should immediately:

▶ **loosen the bandages**; if bleeding starts again, re-tie the bandages

If circulation is still impaired:

▶ **obtain medical help** immediately

Continue checking circulation until hand over to medical help.

Nailbed test

10

You have bandaged a wound on a casualty's arm to maintain control of bleeding. When you recheck for circulation below the point of injury, you note that the hand is colder to the touch than on the uninjured arm and the tips of the fingers stay white when they are compressed.

Check ☑ what you should do for this casualty:

☐ A. Call medical help before doing anything else.

☑ B. Ease the tightness of the bandage and check for good circulation.

☐ C. Rub the fingers to get them as warm as the fingers of the other hand.

☑ D. Tighten the bandages again, if blood shows through the dressings.

☑ E. Call medical help right away if easing up the bandages does not help circulation.

Untying bandage

Care of amputated tissue

11

In many cases amputated parts can be surgically reattached. Proper care of the amputated tissue, therefore, is very important.

For a completely amputated part, you should:

◆ wrap it in a clean, moist dressing, if possible; otherwise a clean and dry dressing

◆ place it in a clean, watertight plastic bag and seal it

◆ place it into another bag with a cold pack or crushed ice to keep it cool

◆ label the bag with the casualty's name, date and the time it was wrapped

◆ take or send the part to medical help with the casualty

For a partially amputated part, you should:

◆ keep it as near as possible to its normal position

◆ cover it with a moist dressing if possible; otherwise a dry dressing. Apply direct pressure on the wound to stop bleeding

◆ secure the dressings in place with a bandage

◆ obtain medical help as soon as possible

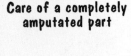

Care of a completely amputated part

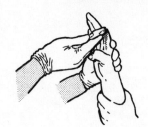

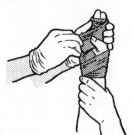
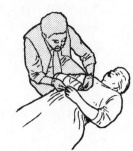

Care of a partially amputated part

12

Select and indicate ☑ the correct completions for the following statements.

A completely amputated part should be:

☑ A. Covered with a sterile, damp gauze, if available.

☐ B. Placed in a container with warm water to maintain body temperature.

☑ C. Sealed in a waterproof container and kept cool.

☐ D. Identified with the name of the first aider and the care given to the casualty.

☑ E. Sent to the hospital with the injured person.

A partially amputated part should be:

☑ F. Kept in its natural place with a dressing and bandage.

☐ G. Kept in place with adhesive tape.

A C E F

First aid for internal bleeding

13

The most important thing, you as a first aider, can do is to:

▶ **recognize** the history and mechanism of injury that might cause internal bleeding

▶ **recognize** shock

▶ give **first aid for shock** to lessen its effects

▶ **obtain prompt medical help**

Shock position

While waiting for medical help, make the casualty as comfortable as possible.

▶ Place the **conscious** casualty at rest on his back with feet and legs elevated to about 30 cm (12 inches), if injuries permit

▶ Place the **unconscious**, breathing casualty into the recovery position

▶ Reassure the casualty

▶ Preserve body heat

▶ Give nothing by mouth

▶ Reassess airway, breathing and circulation

Recovery position

Recovery position covered

14

Which of the following would you do for a conscious casualty with suspected internal bleeding?

Check off ☑ your choices:

☐ A. Tell the casualty that he is bleeding badly inside his body.

☑ B. Obtain medical help quickly.

☑ C. Comfort the casualty with gentle encouragement.

☑ D. Place a blanket under and over the casualty.

☐ E. Allow the casualty to take sips of water.

☑ F. If the condition allows, raise the casualty's lower legs on a folded coat.

Objectives

· ·

Following the videos and upon completion of your practical skills and this activity book exercise, in an emergency situation, you will be able to:

▶ use dressings and bandages in first aid procedures

▶ recognize major wounds

▶ recognize severe external and internal bleeding

▶ provide first aid for wounds with severe external bleeding

▶ provide first aid for amputations and care for amputated tissue

▶ recognize inadequate circulation to the extremities and provide the appropriate first aid

▶ provide first aid for internal bleeding

For further information on first aid for severe bleeding, please refer to:
First on the Scene, the St. John Ambulance first aid and CPR manual, chapter 6, available through your instructor or any major bookstore in your area.

CHILD RESUSCITATION

1

You will recall that for first aid and CPR techniques, a **child** is someone who is **between 1 and 8 years old.**

Cardiovascular disease is not very common in children. However, children can be taught how to prevent cardiovascular disease by learning about healthy food and good living habits.

It is more common for children to suffer **breathing emergencies** caused by disease or injury. Stopped breathing may lead to **cardiac arrest.**

► Breathing must be restored immediately

Suffocation

Some common **causes/mechanisms of injury** for stopped breathing in children are:

- ► injury caused in car collisions
- ► a blocked airway (choking)
- ► suffocation
- ► electric shock
- ► strangulation

- ► near-drowning
- ► smoke inhalation and burns
- ► poisoning
- ► upper respiratory infection
- ► allergies

Anyone who cares for a child should know how to:

- ► **prevent** breathing emergencies, when possible
- ► **recognize** when breathing has stopped
- ► **act immediately** to restore breathing

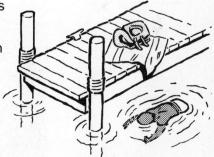

Near drowning

2

Mark each of the following statements as either true **(T)** or false **(F)**:

- ☐ A. Parents, teachers and babysitters should be trained to handle emergency situations.
- ☐ B. Situations which result in stopped breathing in children are very rare.
- ☐ C. A child who is not breathing must receive first aid immediately.
- ☐ D. Many breathing emergencies occur when children are not supervised.

A.T B.F C.T D.T

Prevention of breathing emergencies

3

The best way to protect children is to prevent breathing emergencies from happening! Most breathing emergencies in children can be prevented. **Injuries** are the biggest risk to children.

Small objects

Dangerous food

To help protect children, you should:

▶ use car seats and other child restraints that are properly installed

▶ teach children to be "street smart"

 ▪ how to use roads safely

 ▪ to wear bicycle helmets

Blocked airway by the tongue

Choking is the most common breathing emergency in children. It is usually caused when the airway is blocked by the tongue, food or small objects.

To prevent choking and other breathing emergencies, you should:

▶ place an unconscious, breathing child into the recovery position

▶ supervise young children when they are eating

▶ don't give young children nuts, popcorn, hard candies, etc. to eat

▶ keep small objects such as marbles, toy parts and broken, uninflated balloons away from small children

▶ check toys and household objects for small detachable parts

▶ make sure children use their toys as recommended by the manufacturer

▶ enrol children in swimming lessons to help prevent near-drowning

▶ teach children about the dangers of electricity

▶ keep poisonous products, including medications, out of the reach of children

4

Check ☑ the correct endings for the following statement. To prevent breathing emergencies in children, you should:

☐ A. Keep floors clear of small objects that could be placed in the mouth.

☐ B. Cover electrical outlets in your home.

☐ C. Serve hot dogs in one piece so the young child can hold them better.

☐ D. Teach your children water safety rules early in life.

☐ E. Tell your child that he will learn all about street safety when he goes to school.

A B D

Artificial respiration

. . . .

5

For a child, you should use the **mouth-to-mouth method** of **AR**. Use the same techniques as for an adult, with the following modifications:

◆ give one breath **every 3 seconds**

◆ use slow breaths of air, **just** enough to make the chest rise

◆ take **1 to 1.5 seconds** for each breath

◆ if you are alone, give AR for **about one minute** then go to call for medical help. Carry the child with you and continue with AR, if possible

   ◆ remember, brain damage may result after as little as 4 minutes of stopped breathing

Pulse and breathing rates vary according to the age of the person.

◆ The average **pulse rate** of a healthy child at rest is **80 to 100 beats** per minute

◆ The average, **breathing rate** of a healthy child at rest is about **20 to 30 breaths** per minute

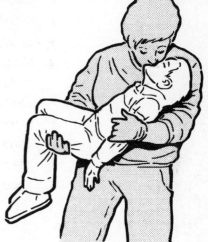

Mouth-to-mouth AR   Check carotid pulse   Carrying child

. . . .

6

Mark each of the following statements as either true **(T)** or false **(F)**:

☐ A. Along with the age, the size of the child should be considered when giving artificial respiration.

☐ B. A breathing rate of 20 breaths per minute is normal for a child.

☐ C. The amount of air required to ventilate a small child is the same as for an adult.

☐ D. When you are alone with a non-breathing child who has a pulse, it is more important to continue AR than to call for an ambulance immediately.

☐ E. The pulse and breathing rates of children and adults are the same.

A.T B.T C.F D.T E.F

Signs of choking and first aid

7

When a child has breathing difficulties caused by swelling of the tissues from an allergy or an infection, get medical help or take the child to the hospital immediately! Do not waste time trying to clear the airway.

When a child is choking, you may see the same signs as in an adult depending on the degree of obstruction. If he can cough effectively, encourage his efforts, stand by, ready to help. A very young child cannot show you, as clearly as an adult, that he has trouble breathing.

Start first aid for choking immediately when you observe:

▶ the child choking on an object

▶ weak, ineffective coughing

▶ breathing becoming faster as the child tries to take in more air or it may become irregular, or may stop for short periods of time

▶ abnormal sounds such as wheezing or high-pitched noises

▶ a bluish tinge to the skin

▶ the child clutching his throat

Universal distress sign of choking

Differences in first aid for choking in children and adults:

▶ landmark and give abdominal thrusts for a conscious child from a position where the shoulders of the first aider and the child are at the same level, e.g. **kneeling position**

▶ do not perform a blind fingersweep for an unconscious child. Remove only what you can see

Remember, a child should always receive medical care following abdominal thrusts. This manoeuvre may cause internal damage.

8

Which of the following conditions might indicate that a child is choking on an object? Check ☑ the correct answers.

☐ A. A child is pale and sweating.

☐ B. A child is gagging at the dinner table.

☐ C. A playing child is eating peanuts and suddenly cannot make a sound.

☐ D. A child has a high temperature and has great difficulty getting air.

☐ E. A young child is staring wide-eyed with his hands on the front part of his neck.

B C E

First aid for choking—review

9

You have seen the videos and practised the first aid for a choking child. You have already done a scene survey and assessed the child as unresponsive. Place the remaining first aid steps in the **order you should perform them**. Write the appropriate numbers into the boxes provided.

☐ A. Landmark and give up to 5 abdominal thrusts.

☐ B. Open the airway and check for breathing (not breathing).

☐ C. Open the mouth using the tongue-jaw lift and look for the object (object expelled).

☐ D. Send a bystander to get medical help.

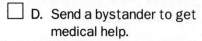

Get medical help!

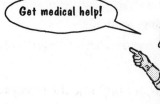

☐ E. Tilt the head backward and try to ventilate the lungs (chest does not rise).

☐ F. Reposition the head. Check the seals at the mouth and nose and try to ventilate (chest does not rise).

A.5 B.2 C.6 D.1 E.3 F.4

Cardiopulmonary resuscitation (CPR)

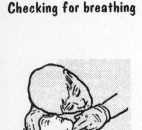

Checking for breathing

10

CPR is two basic life-support skills put together—artificial respiration and artificial circulation.

CPR is used to circulate oxygenated blood to the tissues and maintain the life of a child when –

► breathing has stopped and

► the heart has stopped beating

Differences between adult and child CPR:

► if you are alone, do not go for immediate medical help when you find the child unresponsive

► continue your assessment

► if the child has no pulse, **give CPR for one minute**. Then go for medical help. Carry the child with you, if possible, and continue CPR

► if the child is too heavy, place him into the recovery position before you go for medical help. When you return, reassess breathing and pulse before continuing with CPR

► use only the heel of one hand to give chest compressions

► use a ratio of 5:1 for chest compressions and ventilations

► compress the chest 2.5 to 3.8 cm (1 to 1.5 inches)

► give compressions at a rate of 100 per minute

Checking for pulse

Chest compressions

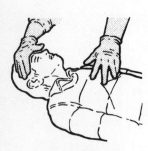

Landmarking

11

Mark each of the following statements as either true **(T)** or false **(F)**:

☐ A. The aim of CPR is to maintain circulation and breathing until hand over to medical help.

☐ B. If breathing has stopped and there is no pulse, you should start CPR immediately.

☐ C. When you find that a child is not reacting when you call out to him or touch him, you should find out if he is breathing and has a pulse.

☐ D. The CPR techniques for a child are the same as for an adult.

☐ E. If you are alone, it is more important to do CPR for one minute than to go for medical help immediately.

A.T B.T C.T D.F E.T

Child CPR—review

12

You have practised the CPR techniques for a child and have seen them performed on the video.

You have already done the scene survey and found that the child is unresponsive. Place the remaining first aid steps in **the order you should perform them when you are alone.** Write the appropriate numbers into the boxes provided.

☐ A. Check for carotid pulse (no pulse).

☐ B. Open the airway using the head-tilt chin-lift.

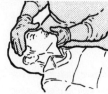

☐ C. Try to give two slow breaths (chest rises).

☐ D. Check for breathing (not breathing).

☐ E. Go for medical help, carrying the child with you and continuing CPR.

☐ F. Landmark for chest compressions.

☐ G. Recheck the pulse and breathing after one minute (not breathing, no pulse).

☐ H. Give cycles of 5 compressions and 1 ventilation for one minute.

A.4 B.1 C.3 D.2 E.8 F.5 G.7 H.6

Objectives

· ·

Following the video and upon completion of your practical skills and this activity book exercise, in an emergency situation, you will be able to:

► take measures to prevent breathing emergencies in children

► perform mouth-to-mouth artificial respiration on a child

► provide first aid for a choking child

► perform one-rescuer CPR on a child

For further information on child resuscitation, please refer to:
First on the Scene, the St. John Ambulance first aid and CPR manual, chapters 3, 4 and 5, available through your instructor or any major bookstore in your area.

EXERCISE 7

INFANT RESUSCITATION

1

As you have learned before, the word **infant** describes a baby **up to 1 year** of age.

When an infant's **heart stops** beating it is usually not caused by a problem in the heart itself. Most often it is the result of a breathing emergency. After a short time without oxygen, the infant's heart will stop beating.

▶ You must give first aid for stopped breathing immediately

Electrocution

The most common **causes/mechanisms of injury** for breathing emergencies in an infant are:

▶ injuries
▶ choking on a foreign object
▶ smoke inhalation
▶ suffocation
▶ infection

▶ allergies
▶ strangulation
▶ electrocution
▶ near-drowning
▶ sudden infant death syndrome (SIDS)

Anyone who cares for an infant should know how to:

▶ **prevent** breathing emergencies, when possible
▶ **recognize** when breathing has stopped
▶ **act immediately** to restore breathing

Suffocation

2

Mark each of the following statements as either true **(T)** or false **(F)**:

☐ A. Most babies stop breathing because of a heart problem.
☐ B. When breathing in a baby is interrupted for some time, the heart will stop working.
☐ C. Airway obstructions rarely happen in babies.
☐ D. Parents, teachers and babysitters responsible for a baby should be trained to handle emergency situations.

A.F B.T C.F D.T

How to prevent breathing emergencies

3

As with children, the best way to protect an infant, is to prevent a breathing emergency!

To protect an infant from injury and breathing emergencies, you should:

► use car seats appropriate for the age of the infant that are properly installed

► use approved gates to close off stairways in your home

► check your child's pacifier. Make sure it is made in one piece

► check all toys for small parts that could break off

► always supervise infants when they are eating

► not leave a baby to feed himself with a propped-up bottle

► pick the baby up and hold him during feeding time

► keep plastic bags away from infants to prevent suffocation

► not leave an infant unattended on an adult waterbed

Small objects

Dangerous food

SIDS—Sudden Infant Death Syndrome

SIDS, also called crib death, is the unexplained death of an apparently healthy infant. The infant dies suddenly and unexpectedly, usually while sleeping. To help reduce the possible risk factors:

► put the baby to sleep on her back or side, on a firm, flat surface

► keep the baby in a smoke-free environment

► do not overheat the baby

► breastfeed the baby, if possible

Parents should not feel that the death of their baby from SIDS is their fault. Research tells us how we may reduce the chances, but we cannot prevent all SIDS deaths. The actual cause of SIDS is still unknown.

The Canadian Foundation for the Study of Infant Deaths, Canadian Institute for Child Health, Canadian Pediatric Society, and Health Canada.

Watch out for possible dangers. Focus on safety!

4

Which of the following would protect your baby from a breathing emergency? Check ☑ the correct statements below.

☐ A. Place hanging mobiles within reach of a baby's hand.

☐ B. Ensure that electrical outlets are covered when the baby starts crawling.

☐ C. Install a smoke detector in each level of your home.

☐ D. Supervise your baby during feeding and play time.

☐ E. There is no need to look in on your baby during his sleep.

Artificial respiration

. . . .

5

For infants and small delicate children you should use the **mouth-to-mouth-and-nose method** of artificial respiration.

Brachial pulse

To use the **mouth-to-mouth-and-nose method**, follow the same procedures as for the mouth-to-mouth method, with the following changes:

◆ make a good seal with your mouth **over the mouth and nose** of the infant

◆ give one breath **every 3 seconds**

◆ use **slow breaths of air**, just enough to make the chest rise

◆ check the **brachial pulse** found on the inside of the upper arm

◆ if alone, give AR for **about one minute**, then go to call for medical help. Carry the infant with you, if possible, and continue AR

   ◆ remember, brain damage may result after as little as 4 minutes of stopped breathing

Mouth-to-mouth-and-nose method

. . . .

6

Which of the following techniques are used when giving AR to an infant or very small child? Check ☑ your answers from the following two choices.

Choice 1	Choice 2
☐ A. Cover the mouth tightly.	☐ A. Cover the mouth and nose tightly.
☐ B. Blow into the mouth and nose with a strong force.	☐ B. Blow into the mouth and nose enough to make the chest move.
☐ C. Give ventilations at a faster rate than for an adult.	☐ C. Give ventilations at the same rate as for an adult.
☐ D. Take the pulse at the neck.	☐ D. Take the pulse on the inside of the upper arm.
☐ E. If you are by yourself, start AR before you call for an ambulance.	☐ E. If you are by yourself, call for an ambulance before you start AR.

A.2 B.2 C.1 D.2 E.1

The brachial pulse

7

To **check if the heart is beating** and pumping blood to the vital organs, you must take the pulse when giving artificial respiration.

To check the **brachial pulse** on an infant:

▶ support the head to keep the airway open

▶ place the fingers on the inside of the upper arm and press lightly between the muscle and the bone to feel the pulse

▶ take 5 to 10 seconds for the first pulse check

▶ after about one minute of AR and every few minutes thereafter, **recheck** the **pulse** and **breathing for 5 seconds**

An **infant's breathing and pulse rates** are faster than an adult's or a child's.

▶ The resting breathing rate of a healthy infant is about **30 to 50 breaths** per minute

▶ The resting pulse rate of a healthy infant is **100 to 140** beats per minute

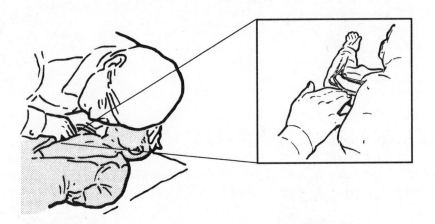

The brachial pulse

8

Mark each of the following statements as either true (**T**) or false (**F**):

☐ A. When giving AR to a baby, you should take the pulse on the inside of the upper arm.

☐ B. Expect a baby's pulse to be slower than that of an adult.

☐ C. To feel the brachial pulse, you would place two finger tips into the armpit.

☐ D. When you are taking the pulse, you should keep the airway open with one hand.

A.T B.F C.F D.T

Infant AR—review

· ·

9

This question is based on the video you have seen, on your practical exercise and this activity book exercise.

Your neighbour calls for you to help. She cannot wake up her baby. Place the first aid procedures below **in the correct order.** Place the appropriate numbers into the boxes provided.

☐ A. Look, listen and feel for breathing.

☐ B. Call out "baby, baby" and tap the infant's feet.

☐ C. Send the mother for medical help.

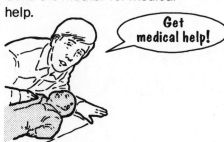

Get medical help!

☐ D. Cover the baby's mouth and nose and attempt to give 2 slow breaths.

☐ E. Open the airway using the head-tilt chin-lift.

☐ F. Give one slow breath every three seconds for about 1 minute.

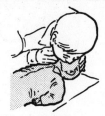

☐ G. Check for a brachial pulse (there is a pulse).

☐ H. Recheck for a pulse and breathing after one minute and again every few minutes.

A.4 B.1 C.2 D.5 E.3 F.7 G.6 H.8

Signs of choking

- -

10

When an infant is choking, **you may see** the same signs as in an adult or child depending on the degree of obstruction.

If an infant **can breathe, cry, or cough forcefully**, the airway is clear. An infant cannot show you, as clearly as an adult, that he has trouble breathing.

Start first aid for choking immediately when you observe:

When an infant has breathing difficulties caused by illness or an allergic reaction, get medical help urgently, or bring the infant to a hospital immediately. Do not waste time trying to clear the airway.

- ▶ the infant choking on an object
- ▶ weak, ineffective coughing
- ▶ breathing becoming faster, irregular or stopping for short periods of time
- ▶ high-pitched noises
- ▶ a bluish tinge to the skin
- ▶ the infant can no longer breathe, cough forcefully or cry

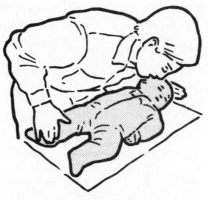

Look for signs of choking

- -

11

Which of the following conditions might indicate that a baby is choking on an object?

Check ☑ the correct answers.

☐ A. A baby has a high temperature and has problems getting air into his lungs.

☐ B. A baby makes harsh, shrill sounds while struggling to breathe.

☐ C. An infant sucking on a pacifier suddenly cannot make a sound.

☐ D. A baby holding his own bottle starts whimpering and gagging.

☐ E. A baby is pale and listless.

First aid for choking

12

When you give **first aid** for a choking infant, you should use the following **differences in procedures**:

▶ always **support** the delicate **head and neck** when holding and turning an infant

▶ **never use abdominal thrusts**

▶ give a combination of **5 back blows and 5 chest thrusts** instead

▶ **check the mouth** using the tongue-jaw lift and remove **only** objects that you can see

▶ **never** make blind finger sweeps

▶ use slow breaths with just enough air to make the chest rise when you try to ventilate

▶ check the brachial pulse

▶ if you are **alone and the infant becomes unconscious,** give about **one minute of first aid** for choking. If the blockage is not relieved, get medical help. Take the baby with you and continue first aid

Remember, a baby should always receive medical care following chest thrusts and back blows to make sure there are no complications

Supporting the baby

Trying to ventilate

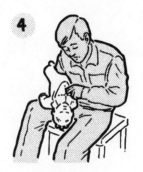

Tongue–jaw lift

Chest thrusts

Back blows

13

Mark each of the following statements as either true **(T)** or false **(F)**.

☐ A. When handling a choking baby, you should protect the fragile head and spine.

☐ B. Give abdominal thrusts to remove the obstruction.

☐ C. Use your fingers to clear the mouth of any material that you can see.

☐ D. Even though the airway is obstructed, you should try to blow with slow breaths through the mouth and nose.

☐ E. If you are alone, call for an ambulance before starting first aid for choking.

A.T B.F C.T D.T E.F

Cardiopulmonary resuscitation (CPR)

Check breathing

Check pulse

14

CPR combines two life-support skills—artificial respiration and artificial circulation.

CPR is used to circulate oxygenated blood to the tissues of an infant when –

► breathing has stopped
► the heart has stopped beating

Differences between adult and infant CPR:

► if you are alone, do not go for medical help when you find an infant unresponsive
► continue your assessment
► if the infant has no pulse, **give CPR for one minute** before going for medical help. Carry the infant with you and continue CPR
► use the brachial pulse
► use only two fingers for chest compressions
► compress the chest only to 1.3 to 2.5 cm (0.5 to 1 inch)
► give compressions at a rate of at least 100 per minute
► use a ratio of 5 compressions to 1 ventilation (5:1)

Chest compressions

Ventilations

15

Mark each of the following statements as either true **(T)** or false **(F)**.

☐ A. The first step to restore breathing is to blow in the nose and mouth.
☐ B. AR is an essential part of CPR.
☐ C. If you are alone with an unresponsive baby, your first step is to call for medical help.
☐ D. If breathing has stopped and there is no pulse, you should start CPR immediately.
☐ E. You should use only one hand to give chest compressions to a baby.

A.F B.T C.F D.T E.F

Infant CPR—review

16

The following question is based on the videos you have seen, your practical exercises and this activity book exercise.

You find your baby unresponsive. You are alone. What first aid actions should you do? Place the first aid procedures shown below in the order you should do them. Write the appropriate numbers into the boxes provided.

☐ A. Landmark and give compressions and ventilations for one minute.

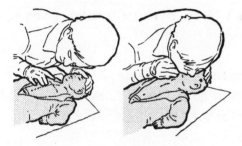

☐ B. Check for a brachial pulse (no pulse).

☐ C. Open the airway and check for breathing (not breathing).

☐ D. Try to give two slow breaths.

☐ E. Get medical help. Carry the baby and continue CPR.

☐ F. Recheck pulse and breathing after one minute (not breathing, no pulse).

A.4 B.3 C.1 D.2 E.6 F.5

Objectives

• •

Following the video and upon completion of your practical skills and this activity book exercise, in an emergency situation, you will be able to:

▶ take measures to prevent breathing emergencies in infants

▶ perform mouth-to-mouth-and-nose artificial respiration on an infant

▶ provide first aid for a choking infant

▶ perform one-rescuer CPR on a infant

For further information on infant resuscitation, please refer to:
First on the Scene, the St. John Ambulance first aid and CPR manual, chapters 3, 4 and 5, available through your instructor or any major bookstore in your area.

. . . .

CARDIOVASCULAR EMERGENCIES
AND ONE RESCUER CPR—ADULT

The heart

. . . .

1

The **heart** acts as a pump. It continuously circulates blood to the lungs and all parts of the body. To do this work, it needs a steady supply of blood rich in oxygen and nutrients.

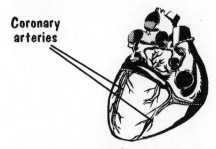

Coronary arteries

Healthy heart

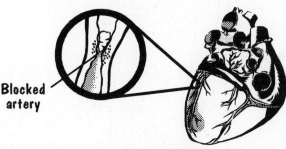

Blocked artery

Damaged heart

Two **coronary arteries** supply this blood to the heart muscle. If the coronary arteries or their branches become narrowed or blocked, a part of the heart will not receive the oxygen it needs. This will cause a cardiovascular emergency.

. . . .

2

Mark each of the following statements as either true **(T)** or false **(F)**.

☐ A. When the body is at rest, the heart does not require oxygen.

☐ B. The heart sends blood to all parts of the body.

☐ C. Special blood vessels provide oxygenated blood to the heart tissue.

☐ D. A heart problem results when part of the heart muscle does not receive enough blood supply.

A.F B.T C.T D.T

Risk factors

. . . .

3

A **risk factor** is a behaviour or trait that increases the chance of someone developing cardiovascular disease. Some risk factors can be controlled, while others cannot.

Cardiovascular risk factors	
Can be controlled	**Cannot be controlled**
Cigarette smoking	A person's
Elevated blood cholesterol	– Age
Elevated blood pressure	– Gender
Diabetes	– Family history
Obesity	
Lack of exercise	
Excessive stress	

The risk of developing a cardiovascular disease can be reduced considerably by adopting a healthy lifestyle.

. . . .

4

Check ☑ the healthy lifestyle habits that can help control the risk of cardiovascular disease.

☐ A. Ensure a non-smoking environment for yourself and your family.

☐ B. Start an exercise program after consultation with your doctor.

☐ C. Eat food high in fat and calories.

☐ D. Have blood pressure checks by a health professional on a regular basis.

☐ E. Maintain a recommended body weight.

☐ F. Take time to relax and rest.

☐ G. Smoke a pipe instead of cigarettes.

Instructor-led exercise 8A

. . . .

5

CARDIOVASCULAR DISEASE

High blood pressure (Hypertension)

1. _____ is the pressure of blood pushing against the inside walls of the blood vessels.

2. A person is said to have high blood pressure when his blood pressure is _____ above normal.

3. Two effects of high blood pressure are:

    a) The walls of the blood vessels become _____ .

    b) The heart becomes _____ .

4. The casualty with high blood pressure **always/almost never** shows signs and symptoms. *(Circle your choice.)*

Narrowing of Arteries (Atherosclerosis)

5. Narrowing of arteries is caused by a build up of _____ on the inside lining.

6. The process of fat being deposited in the arteries begins: *(Circle your choice.)*
    a) when angina begins   b) in childhood   c) in middle age.

7. In the coronary arteries the build up of fatty deposits results in _____ .

Narrowed artery

Angina

8. Angina is a short-lived pain usually felt in the: *(Circle the correct answers.)*
    a) chest   b) neck   c) shoulders   d) jaw   e) hips   f) arms

9. Angina occurs when the heart does not get enough _____ to meet its needs.

10. The most common reason the heart does not get enough oxygen is that the arteries have become _____ .

Instructor-led exercise 8A (cont'd)

5

Blocked artery

Heart attack

11. A heart attack is most often caused by a _____ blocking a coronary artery that is already narrowed. The blood clot blocks the flow of blood to the _____ .

12. Part of the heart muscle dies because it does not get the _____ it needs.

13. A heart attack often feels similar to _____ .

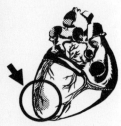

Damaged heart

Cardiac arrest

14. Cardiac arrest means that the heart has stopped _____ .

15. Cardiac arrest is also called

_____ .

16. Common causes of cardiac arrest are:

a) _____   d) _____

b) _____   e) _____

c) _____   f) _____

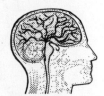

Healthy brain

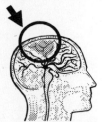

Damaged brain

Ruptured vessel

Stroke

17. A stroke is a condition in which part of the brain tissue dies because of a shortage of _____ .

18. A stroke can be caused by:

a) a _____ in the circulation of blood to the brain; **or**

Blocked vessel

b) a ruptured blood vessel in the _____ .

19. A transient ischemic attack (TIA), is a condition similar to a stroke. It is often called a "mini stroke". A TIA is of short duration and leaves no permanent damage. A TIA is a warning sign that a _____ may follow.

Advise anyone who has a TIA to seek medical help.

Angina/heart attack

6

Angina results from a temporary shortage of oxygen to the heart muscle. The signs and symptoms of angina are similar to a heart attack, except that they are often brought on by physical effort or stress and should be relieved by medication and rest. There is no heart damage in angina as there is in a heart attack.

Signs and symptoms of a heart attack

The casualty may **deny** that he is having a heart attack but you may recognize some or all of the following:

You may see:

▶ shortness of breath

▶ paleness, sweating, and other signs of shock

▶ vomiting

▶ unconsciousness

Pain in arm

Shortness of breath

The casualty may complain of:

▶ crushing chest pain which may or may not be severe

▶ pain spreading to neck, jaw, shoulders and/or arms

▶ shortness of breath

▶ fear, feeling of doom

▶ feeling of indigestion

▶ nausea

Nausea

If some or all of these signs and symptoms are present, a cardiac arrest may follow. Most heart attack deaths occur within the first two hours of the onset of signs and symptoms.

7

Which of the following signs and symptoms might help you to recognize angina or a heart attack? Check ☑ your answers from the listing below.

☐ A. A tingling sensation in the hands and feet.

☐ B. Breathing difficulty.

☐ C. Discomfort in the heart region.

☐ D. The casualty's insistence that it is just a stomach upset.

☐ E. A flushed face.

☐ F. White, moist skin.

☐ G. The casualty is frightened.

B C D F G

First aid for angina/heart attack

Get medical help!

8

The first aid for angina and heart attack is the same.

Your aims for all cardiovascular emergencies are to:

▶ get medical help quickly

▶ reduce the workload of the heart

▶ prevent the casualty's condition from worsening

When you suspect that a person is having a heart attack or angina:

▶ get medical help **immediately**

▶ place the person at rest in the position of most comfort, usually **semisitting**, to ease the work of the heart and help breathing

▶ loosen tight clothing at the neck, chest and waist

▶ reassure the casualty

▶ assist the casualty to take prescribed medication, if requested

Assess breathing. If breathing fails, begin AR immediately.
Assess the pulse. If the pulse stops, begin CPR.

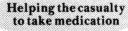
Helping the casualty to take medication

Only assist a casualty with medication if he is fully conscious and specifically requests your help.

Always check the five "rights" before assisting with medications:

▶ *right medication*

▶ *right person*

▶ *right amount*

▶ *right time*

▶ *right method*

9

A middle aged man collapses after running for a bus. He is pale and sweating, is clutching his chest, but is fully conscious. You suspect a heart attack. Which choice of action should you take?

Check ☑ your choices.

Choice 1	**Choice 2**
☐ A. Help him into his house.	☐ A. Send someone to call for an ambulance.
☐ B. Prop up his head and shoulders with your coat.	☐ B. Raise his legs with your coat.
☐ C. If he asks you, help him take his prescribed medicine.	☐ C. Give him plenty of water to drink.
☐ D. Tell him there is nothing to worry about.	☐ D. Speak to him gently and tell him help is on the way.
☐ E. Provide AR and CPR if required.	☐ E. Leave him as dead if breathing or the heart stops.

A.2 B.1 C.1 D.2 E.1

Cardiac arrest

10

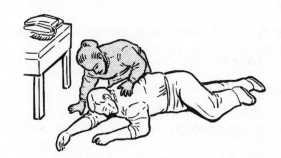

Signs of a cardiac arrest

You will note:

▶ unresponsiveness
▶ no breathing
▶ bluish colour
▶ no pulse

First aid for a suspected cardiac arrest

▶ Perform ESM
▶ Check ABC — airway, breathing and circulation (pulse)
▶ If there is no breathing and no pulse, **start cardiopulmonary resuscitation (CPR) immediately**

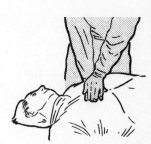

CPR is a combination of two life-support techniques, **artificial respiration** and **artificial circulation.**

The chain of survival

CPR is important, but it is only one of the five steps in the **chain of survival**. Each link is as important as the others. You, the first trained person on the scene, are the crucial first three links in the chain of survival:

▶ **early recognition** of a cardiovascular emergency
▶ **early access** to emergency medical services (EMS); this means calling for help quickly
▶ **early CPR**
▶ **early defibrillation** given by emergency personnel
▶ **early advanced care** given by medical personnel

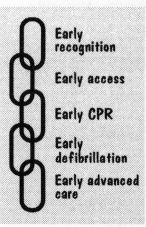

Early recognition

Early access

Early CPR

Early defibrillation

Early advanced care

11

From the options below, choose ☑ the condition which requires that you give CPR:

☐ A. The casualty is unresponsive but is breathing.
☐ B. The casualty is not breathing and has no pulse.
☐ C. The casualty is not breathing but has a pulse.
☐ D. The casualty is choking and has difficulty breathing.

B

Signs and symptoms of stroke

. . . .

12

The signs and symptoms of stroke differ depending on what part of the brain was damaged. You may note some or all of the following:

You may see:

▶ decrease in the casualty's level of consciousness

▶ paralysis of facial muscles

▶ difficulty in speaking and swallowing, e.g. slurred speech, drooling

▶ unsteadiness or a sudden fall

▶ loss of coordination

▶ loss of bladder and bowel control

▶ unequal size of pupils

Unequal size of pupils

The casualty may complain of:

▶ numbness or weakness of arms or legs, especially on one side

▶ severe headache

Paralysis of
facial muscles
(drooping of face)

. . . .

13

Check ☑ the signs and symptoms which could indicate that a stroke has occurred.

☐ A. The casualty wants to talk to you but cannot seem to get the words out.

☐ B. The casualty cannot move his left arm or leg.

☐ C. The casualty appears to be overactive and vomits.

☐ D. The casualty cannot control his need to urinate or move his bowels.

☐ E. When you check the pupils, they are the same size.

☐ F. You notice that the muscles on one side of the face are drooping.

First aid for stroke

14

When you suspect that a person has had a stroke, you should **obtain medical help immediately.** Hospital treatment within one hour of the onset of symptoms will greatly increase the casualty's chances for recovery.

While waiting for medical help, you should:

▶ maintain adequate breathing and circulation

▶ protect him from injury

▶ reassure the casualty

▶ make him as comfortable as possible

▶ loosen tight clothing

If the person is **conscious:**

▶ place him at rest and support him in a **semisitting** position, unless the casualty has a weakness to one side of the body which prevents a semisitting position

▶ moisten his lips and tongue with a wet cloth, if he complains of thirst

If the person is **unconscious:**

▶ place him into the **recovery position** on the paralysed or weakened side to ease breathing

▶ give him nothing by mouth

If breathing stops, begin AR immediately. If the heart stops, give CPR.

15

A middle-aged man suddenly becomes paralysed on his left side. He is conscious and has difficulty speaking. You suspect he has had a stroke.

Check ☑ the correct first aid actions you should take:

☐ A. Instruct someone to call for an ambulance.

☐ B. Tell him to speak clearly.

☐ C. Unbutton his shirt at the neck and loosen his belt.

☐ D. Give him a glass of water to drink.

☐ E. Position him on his left side to help his breathing.

☐ F. Take care to avoid further damage to his body.

A C E F

Cardiovascular emergencies—review

16

Blocked blood vessel

1. Depending on its location in the body, a blood vessel that is narrowed but not completely blocked, is most likely to cause which of the following cardiovascular emergencies?
   Check ☑ your answers.

   ☐ A. TIA (transient ischemic attack—little stroke)

   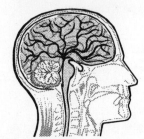

   ☐ B. Stroke

   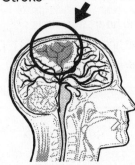

   ☐ C. Heart attack

   ☐ D. Angina

2. You have found a casualty who is not breathing and has no pulse. Which of the following illustrations shows part of the correct first aid procedures?
   Check ☑ your answer.

   ☐ A.   ☐ B.   ☐ C.

   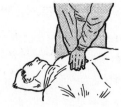

Cardiovascular emergencies—review
Instructor-led exercise 8B

17

What is happening	Signs & symptoms	First aid
Angina/Heart attack	A3. Pain in the _____.	A6. Perform a _____.
A1. The heart muscle is not getting enough blood through the coronary arteries to _____ _____.	A4. Pain may _____.	A7. Perform a _____.
	A5. Any of the following: _____, fear, paleness, nausea, _____, indigestion, shortness of breath, unconsciousness, cardiac arrest.	A8. _____ for medical help.
Heart attack		A9. Place the casualty at rest in a comfortable position. Loosen tight clothing.
A2. Part of the heart muscle is not getting enough blood through the coronary arteries to keep the _____ _____.		A10. If requested, help the _____ casualty to take prescribed medication.
		A11. Give ongoing casualty care until _____.
Cardiac arrest	B2. Unconsciousness.	B5. Begin with a _____.
B1. The heart has _____ and is not _____ any blood.	B3. There is no _____.	B6. Assess _____.
	B4. There is no _____.	B7. _____ for medical help.
		B8. Continue with a primary survey and start _____.
Stroke	C3. _____ in level of consciousness.	C10. Perform a _____.
C1. A part of the _____ is not getting enough blood to function properly. With a stroke, brain tissue _____.	C4. _____ of unequal size.	C11. Perform a _____.
	C5. Hard to _____ and/or swallow.	C12. _____ for medical help.
TIA	C6. Numb or _____ arm or leg.	C13. Place the casualty at rest in a _____ position. _____ tight clothing.
C2. A part of the brain is not getting enough blood to function properly. With TIA, brain tissue _____ _____.	C7. Mental confusion.	C14. Give _____ by mouth.
	C8. Convulsions.	C15. _____ the casualty during movement or convulsions.
	C9. The signs and symptoms of a _____ are not long lasting.	C16. If unconscious, place in _____ position, _____ side down.
Answers: Addendum A		C17. Give ongoing casualty care until _____.

Objectives

• •

Following the videos and upon completion of your practical skills and this activity book exercise, in an emergency situation you will be able to:

▶ apply the knowledge of cardiovascular disease

▶ apply the knowledge of risk factors of cardiovascular disease

▶ apply the knowledge of preventive health measures

▶ apply the principles of first aid for cardiovascular emergencies

▶ recognize angina/heart attack and provide first aid

▶ recognize a cardiac arrest

▶ perform one-rescuer cardiopulmonary resuscitation (CPR) on an adult casualty

▶ recognize a stroke/TIA and provide first aid

For further information on cardiovascular emergencies and CPR, please refer to: *First on the Scene*, the St. John Ambulance first aid and CPR manual, chapters 5 and 11, available through your instructor or any major bookstore in your area.

SECONDARY SURVEY

10 min

1

Once you have given first aid for life-threatening conditions, you may need to do a secondary survey.

A secondary survey should be done when:

► medical help is delayed

► the casualty tells you about more than one area of pain

► you must transport the casualty to a hospital

The secondary survey is a step by step gathering of information which will help you to get a complete picture of the condition of the casualty.

The secondary survey consists of four steps that you should do in the following order:

1. obtain the history of the casualty

2. assess and record vital signs

3. perform a head-to-toe examination

4. give first aid for injuries and illnesses found

2

Mark each of the following statements relating to the secondary survey as either true **(T)** or false **(F)**:

☐ A. You do a secondary survey to discover any immediate danger to the casualty's life.

☐ B. Before you transport a casualty, you should check each part of his body carefully for signs of injuries.

☐ C. The steps of the secondary survey can be done in any sequence that is convenient.

☐ D. With the secondary survey you can find out details about the person's injuries and illnesses.

A.F B.T C.F D.T

3

History of the casualty

By taking the history of a casualty, you are trying to find out everything that is important about the casualty's condition.

A simple way to ensure that you take a complete history of the casualty, is to remember the word **SAMPLE,** where each letter stands for a part of the history:

S = symptoms

A = allergies

M = medications

P = past and present medical history

L = last meal

E = events leading to the incident

▶ **Ask the conscious casualty** how she feels now. Be guided by the casualty's complaints

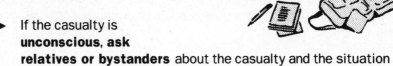

Where do you hurt?

▶ If the casualty is **unconscious, ask relatives or bystanders** about the casualty and the situation

How do you feel?

Check the neck, wrist or ankles for a **medical alert device** (*see next page*)

4

If you want to find out about the history of the casualty, which of the following actions should you do?

Check ☑ the correct answers.

☐ A. Ask the conscious casualty where she feels pain at the moment.

☐ B. Question witnesses about what happened to the unresponsive casualty.

☐ C. Find out about the casualty's past history to help you give appropriate first aid.

☐ D. Ask bystanders what first aid to give.

A B C

Medical alert information

. . . .

5

A **medical alert** device, e.g. a **bracelet, necklace, anklet or pocket card** contains valuable information about the medical history of a casualty. Sometimes this information is kept in a specially marked container on the top shelf of the **person's refrigerator.** Look on the refrigerator door for directions.

When examining an **unconscious** casualty **look for medical alert information.** It may help you in your assessment and in giving appropriate first aid. Some medical alert devices give a phone number where more information about the casualty can be obtained.

A medical alert device may **warn you** that a person wearing it –

▶ has a **medical condition** needing special treatment
   or
▶ is **allergic** to certain substances, e.g. medications, foods, insect bites, plants

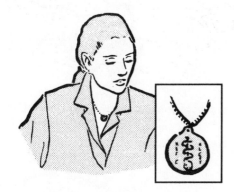

Medical alert necklace

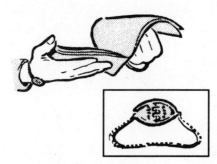

Medical alert bracelet

. . . .

6

Mark each of the following statements as either true **(T)** or false **(F)**:

☐ A. Important facts that may affect the condition of a casualty may be revealed on a medical alert device.

☐ B. Medical-alert jewellery may be worn by a person whose arm swells and who has difficulty breathing after a bee sting.

☐ C. Medical alert information will tell you the age of the casualty.

☐ D. You should also search for medical alert information on every conscious casualty.

A.T B.T C.F D.F

7

Vital signs

The **vital signs** are important indicators of a casualty's condition. The four vital signs you will learn about are:

1. level of consciousness
2. breathing
3. pulse
4. skin condition

You should note and record the vital signs as a basis for further assessments.

Levels of consciousness (LOC)		
When a person is **conscious**	When a person is **semi-conscious**	When a person is **unconscious**

Eye opening response

eyes open spontaneously

eyes open to speech or pain

eyes don't open

Verbal response

he is oriented and alert

he is confused, doesn't make sense

he is not aware of his surroundings

Motor response

he obeys commands

he reacts to pain

he doesn't react to pain

Any serious injury or illness can affect consciousness.

Levels of consciousness (cont'd)

Refer to chart with LOC on page 10 – 4

How to assess the level of consciousness

(Modified Glasgow Coma Scale)

You assess a person's level of consciousness by rating three of his responses:

1. **Eye opening response**	2. **Best verbal response**	3. **Best motor response**

"Open your eyes"	"What time is it?"	"Move your fingers"

Any changes in the level of consciousness should be noted and recorded.

8

Match each casualty's description with a level of consciousness by writing the appropriate number into the squares provided.

Casualty

☐ A. A woman is lying on the street. She opens her eyes only when you talk to her, but is unable to tell you her name and where she lives.

☐ B. A child has fallen off his bicycle and is lying on the ground. As you approach, he starts to cry and reaches for his bicycle.

☐ C. After calling out to a man found lying on the floor and tapping his shoulders, he neither opens his eyes, nor answers.

Levels of consciousness

1. Conscious
2. Semi-conscious
3. Unconscious

A.2 B.1 C.3

9

How to assess breathing

In your primary survey, you determined that the casualty is breathing. Now you should check if the breathing is **effective** or **ineffective**.

If the casualty is conscious:

▶ **look** at the casualty's chest/abdomen and **ask:** "Is your breathing O.K.?"

▶ **listen** to how well the casualty answers and **note** the quality (rate, rhythm and depth) of breathing

If the casualty has difficulty responding, cannot respond, or **is unconscious**:

▶ **place** a hand on the chest of the casualty and

▶ **check the rate, rhythm and depth of breathing**

Normal, effective breathing is quiet and effortless with an even steady rhythm. Check for:

▶ **rate** – is the number of breaths per minute within the normal range?

▶ **rhythm** – are the pauses between breaths of even length?

▶ **depth** – is the breathing shallow, too deep or gasping and noisy?

The following table gives breathing rates for all ages. If a casualty's breathing is too slow or too fast, assist breathing with artificial respiration; see page 3 – 7 in this activity book.

Breathing rate — breaths per minute			
age group	range of normal rates	too slow	too fast
adult (over 8 yrs.)	10 to 20	below 10	above 30
child (1 to 8 yrs.)	20 to 30	below 15	above 40
infant (under 1 yr.)	30 to 50	below 25	above 60

10

From the examples below, check ☑ the signs that could help you determine if a casualty needs help with breathing.

☐ A. The casualty says that her breathing is fine.

☐ B. Breathing becomes laboured and noisy.

☐ C. The pauses between breaths change from very short to very long.

☐ D. Breathing is smooth and regular.

11

How to assess the pulse

The pulse is the pressure wave with each beat of the heart that is felt at different parts of the body. By taking the pulse you check that the heart is beating and blood is circulating throughout the body.

When assessing the pulse, note the:

◆ **rate** – how many times does the heart beat in a minute?

◆ **rhythm** – are the pauses regular between the pulse beats?

◆ **strength** – are the pulse beats strong or weak?

The carotid pulse

Normal pulse rates, by age	
age	rates (heartbeats per min.)
adult (8 and over)	50 to 100
child (1 to 8)	80 to 100
infant (under 1 yr.)	100 to 140

The pulse of a healthy adult at rest varies from 50 to 100 beats , **averaging about 72 beats per** minute, is strong, and has a regular rhythm.

Never use your thumb

to take a pulse—it has

a pulse of its own and

you may feel it instead

of the casualty's pulse.

How to determine your own pulse rate carotid/radial:	
1. Feel your pulse	
2. Count the number of beats for 30 seconds	
3. Multiply by 2	x 2
4. The result is **your pulse rate**	

Pulse rates for an adult at rest (beats per minute)

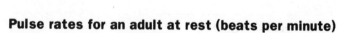

slow	normal range	fast
40 50 60	70 72 80 90	100 110 120

↑
average

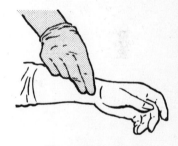

The radial pulse

Does your pulse rate fall within the **normal** range for an adult?

12

Mark the following statements regarding the pulse as either true **(T)** or false **(F)**:

☐ A. The presence of a pulse indicates that the person is breathing normally.

☐ B. The radial pulse can be checked on either wrist.

☐ C. The pulse can be taken on more than one location of the body.

☐ D. A pulse count of 68 beats per minute in a resting adult casualty is within a normal range.

A.F B.T C.T D.T

13

Skin condition and temperature

The condition and temperature of the skin change when there is shock. Checking skin condition and temperature will help you to find out if the casualty is in shock.

How to assess skin condition

▶ check the skin for colour –
  ■ is it pale, reddish or bluish?
▶ check for presence of sweat –
  ■ is the skin clammy or dry?

place the back of your hand on the forehead, neck or cheek

pull back your glove if necessary to feel change of temperature

How to assess skin temperature

▶ use the back of your hand which is more sensitive to feel –
  ■ is the skin warm, hot or cool?
  ■ is the skin dry or wet?

Reassess the vital signs every few minutes or when you think the casualty's condition has changed. Write down your findings and the time of each observation.

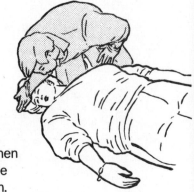

14

From the choices below, check ☑ the correct answer to the following question.

When assessing skin condition and temperature, which one of the following groups of signs would indicate shock (inadequate circulation to body tissues)?

☐ A. Red, hot and dry skin.
☐ B. Pale, cold and clammy skin.
☐ C. Red, hot and sweaty skin.
☐ D. Bluish, cold and dry skin.

Head-to-toe examination—review

· ·

15

The following question is based on the video and your practical exercise.

In the secondary survey you should examine a casualty from head-to-toe for less obvious injuries and illnesses. What sequence in the **top-down approach** would you follow to ensure a **thorough, systematic** examination of the casualty?

Place the illustrations **in the order** you have learned to do the head-to-toe examination by writing the appropriate number into the squares provided:

☐ A. Check the neck.

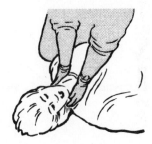

☐ B. Check the head.

☐ C. Check the shoulders, arms and hands.

☐ D. Check the chest and under.

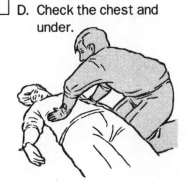

☐ E. Check both collar-bones.

☐ F. Check the pelvis and buttocks.

☐ G. Check the abdomen and under.

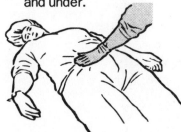

☐ H. Check the legs, ankles and feet.

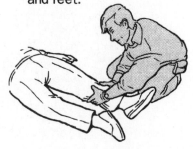

Give first aid for injuries and illnesses found.

A.2 B.1 C.4 D.5 E.3 F.7 G.6 H.8

Objectives

Following the video and upon completion of your practical skills and this activity book exercise, in an emergency situation, you will be able to:

▶ perform the four steps of a secondary survey:

- obtain the history of the casualty

- assess and record vital signs

- perform a head-to-toe examination

- give first aid for non life-threatening conditions

For further information on the secondary survey, please refer to:
First on the Scene, the St. John Ambulance first aid and CPR manual, chapter 2, available through your instructor or any major bookstore in your area.

EXERCISE 11

BONE & JOINT INJURIES
—UPPER LIMBS; MUSCLE STRAINS

Fractures

1

A basic knowledge of the structure of the upper limbs will help you to give first aid for injuries to these parts of the body.

A **fracture** is any break or crack in a bone.

A fracture may be **closed** or **open**

► **Closed fracture** – a fracture where **the skin is not broken**

► **Open fracture** – a fracture where **the skin is broken** and **bone ends may protrude**

The cause/mechanism of injury for upper limb fractures may be:

► **direct force**, e.g. a hard blow or kick

► **indirect force**, e.g. the bone breaks at some distance from the point of impact

► **twisting**, e.g. abnormal turning (rotation) of shoulder or wrist joint

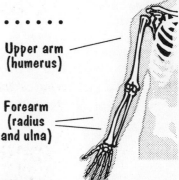

Upper arm (humerus)

Forearm (radius and ulna)

Upper limb

Closed fracture

2

Mark each of the following statements as either true **(T)** or false **(F)**.

☐ A. There is one long bone between the shoulder and the elbow.

☐ B. There are two separate, long bones between the elbow and the wrist.

☐ C. A cracked bone over which the skin is swollen is considered an open fracture.

☐ D. A fracture over which a bleeding wound is seen is a closed fracture.

☐ E. A broken collarbone that results from a fall on the outstretched arm is caused by indirect force.

Open fracture

A.T B.T C.F D.F E.T

Joint injuries

. . . .

3

A **joint** is formed where two or more bones come together. Joints allow for body movement. The bones of a joint are held in place by supporting tissue called **ligaments**.

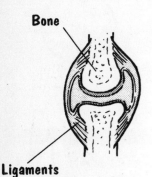

Bone

Ligaments

Joint with supporting tissue (ligaments)

The major joints of the upper limb are at the:

▶ shoulder
▶ elbow
▶ wrist

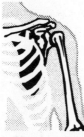 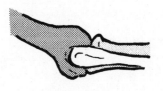 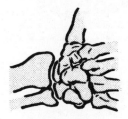

Shoulder joint   **Elbow joint**   **Wrist joint**

Joint injuries happen when the bones and surrounding tissues are forced to move beyond their normal range.

Two common joint injuries are **sprains** and **dislocations**:

▶ **sprain** – a complete or partial tearing or stretching of the ligaments around a joint
▶ **dislocation** – a displacement of one or more bone ends at a joint so that their surfaces are no longer in proper contact

. . . .

4

Mark each of the following statements as either true **(T)** or false **(F)**.

☐ A. A joint is where two or more bones meet.
☐ B. Tissues surrounding the bones of a joint prevent its movement.
☐ C. A sprain occurs when the supporting tissues around a joint are over-stretched or damaged.
☐ D. A dislocation occurs when the bones at a joint are pushed out of their position.

A.T B.F C.T D.T

General signs and symptoms

5

Some or all of the following signs and symptoms occur in most bone and joint injuries –

You may see:

► swelling and discolouration
► deformity and irregularity
► protruding bone ends
► inability to use the limb
► guarding and tensing of muscles around the injured area
► grating noise that can be heard as the bone ends rub together
► signs of shock, increasing with the severity of the injury

The casualty may complain of:

► pain made worse by movement
► tenderness on touching

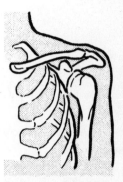

Dislocated shoulder

Deformity and swelling of the shoulder

Open fracture of the humerus

Shoulder dislocation

6

Which of the following could indicate a bone or joint injury of the upper limb?

Check ☑ the correct answers.

☐ A. A cut on the upper arm is bleeding profusely.
☐ B. The end of a bone is sticking through the skin of the forearm.
☐ C. A casualty is pale and sweating. His skin feels cold and his shoulder is in an unnatural position.
☐ D. A casualty cannot bend his elbow and screams when you touch it.
☐ E. A hockey player has fallen and has a painful, swollen wrist.

B   C   D   E

Principles of first aid

7

The **aims of first aid** for bone and joint injuries are:

◆ to prevent further damage and reduce pain

The first aid principles to be followed are:

For any closed fracture, sprain or dislocation, keep the casualty as comfortable as possible with:

◆ *R – Rest*
◆ *I – Ice*
◆ *C – Compression/ bandaging*
◆ *E – Elevation*

◆ perform a scene survey
◆ do a primary survey and give first aid for life-threatening injuries
◆ treat the injury at the incident site, if possible
◆ control bleeding from open wounds, if present
◆ if medical help is close by, **steady and support the injured part** in the position of greatest comfort
◆ apply a cold compress, a wrapped, cold pack or ice bag on any closed fracture or injury to reduce pain and control swelling (15 minutes on – 15 minutes off)
◆ apply gentle pressure/compression with a bandage to reduce swelling
◆ elevate the injured part, if possible
◆ monitor the casualty closely for any change in his condition
◆ reassure the casualty
◆ do not give anything to eat or drink
◆ give ongoing casualty care until hand over

Note: ◆ All fractures, dislocations and sprains should be immobilized before the casualty is moved, unless the casualty is in immediate danger

◆ Always immobilize in the position found.

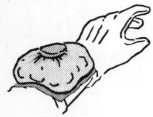

8

Match each situation with the first aid procedure you should perform. Place the appropriate number into the boxes provided:

First aid procedures	Situations
☐ A. Splinting	1. Medical help is readily available.
☐ B. Steady and support	2. A wound over the fracture site is bleeding.
☐ C. Expose and bandage	3. You have to transport the casualty to the hospital.

Splinting

Expose and bandage

A.3 B.1 C.2

Muscle strains

9

A **strain** is an injury that occurs when a muscle is stretched beyond its normal limits.

The cause/mechanism of injury for a strain may be:

▶ sudden pulling or twisting of a muscle

▶ poor body mechanics during lifting

▶ failure to condition muscles before physical activity

▶ repetitive, long-term overuse

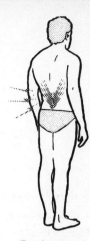

Back strain

A strain can be recognized by some or all of the following –

You may see:

▶ swelling of muscle

▶ discolouration

The casualty may complain of:

▶ sudden sharp pain

▶ severe cramps

▶ stiffness

Signs and symptoms may not appear until later.

**Position of comfort
and cold application
for back strain**

To give first aid, you should:

▶ place the casualty in the position of greatest comfort

▶ apply cold (15 minutes on – 15 minutes off) to help relax muscle spasm, reduce pain and prevent further tissue swelling

▶ refer to medical help

Repetitive strain injury (RSI) is a term that refers to a number of injuries, including back injuries, joint injuries, tennis elbow and bursitis. It is caused by long-term overuse of some joints, muscles and support tissue.

Position of comfort

To give first aid:

▶ keep the casualty as comfortable as possible with

▶ rest, ice, compression and elevation—think RICE

▶ refer to medical help

Prevention: Work breaks, exercises, relaxation techniques, observing proper posture and use of personal protective equipment (wrist/back supports) are the keys to preventing repetitive strain injury.

RICE

R — rest
I — ice
C — compression/
     bandaging
E — elevation

10

Mark each of the following statements as either true **(T)** or false **(F)**.

☐ A. A strain is damage to any of the body's joints.

☐ B. Back strain can be caused by improper carrying techniques.

☐ C. Use of an ice pack and rest is effective treatment for a back strain.

☐ D. A strained leg muscle may cause pain several hours later.

A.F B.T C.T D.T

Objectives

· ·

Following the videos and upon completion of your practical skills and this activity book exercise, in an emergency situation, you will be able to:

▶ recognize bone and joint injuries

▶ provide first aid for bone and joint injuries of the upper limbs

▶ recognize muscle strain and provide first aid

▶ recognize repetitive strain injury and provide first aid

For further information on bone and joint injuries of the upper limbs, and muscle strains, please refer to: *First on the Scene*, the St. John Ambulance first aid and CPR manual, chapter 7, available through your instructor or any major bookstore in your area.

BONE & JOINT INJURIES

—LOWER LIMBS

6 min

Fractures

1

A basic knowledge of the structure of the lower limbs will help you to give first aid for injuries to these parts of the body.

A **fracture** is any break or crack in a bone.

A fracture may be **closed** or **open**:

▶ **Closed fracture** – a fracture where **the skin is not broken**

▶ **Open fracture** – a fracture where **the skin is broken** and **bone ends may protrude**

The cause/mechanism of injury for lower limb fractures may be:

▶ **direct force**, e.g. a powerful force, a hard blow, a kick or a fall, especially in the elderly

▶ **indirect force**, e.g. hip fracture caused by knees forcefully striking the dashboard of a car; fracture to the kneecap caused by powerful muscle contraction

▶ **twisting**, e.g. abnormal turning (rotation) of knee or ankle—occurs in skiing or football incidents

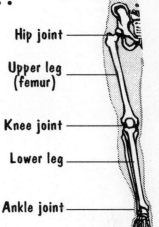

Hip joint

Upper leg (femur)

Knee joint

Lower leg

Ankle joint

Lower limb

2

Mark each of the following statements as either true **(T)** or false **(F)**:

- [ ] A. There is one long bone between the hip and the knee.
- [ ] B. There are two separate, long bones between the knee and the ankle.
- [ ] C. A cracked bone over which the skin is swollen is considered an open fracture.
- [ ] D. A fracture from which a bone end is sticking out is a closed fracture.
- [ ] E. The thigh bone may be broken anywhere along its length.

Closed fracture of the upper leg (femur)

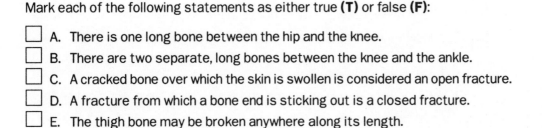

Open fracture of the lower leg (tibia)

A.T B.T C.F D.F E.T

Joint injuries

3

A **joint** is formed where two or more bones come together. Joints allow for body movement. The bones of a joint are held in place by supporting tissue called **ligaments.**

The major joints of the lower limb are at the:

▶ hip
▶ knee
▶ ankle

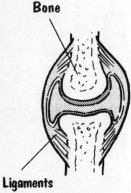

Bone

Ligaments

Joint with supporting tissue (ligaments)

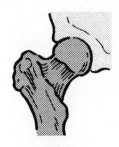

Hip joint

Knee joint

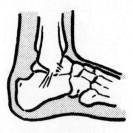

Ankle joint

Joint injuries happen when the bones and surrounding tissues are forced to move beyond their normal range.

Two common joint injuries are **sprains** and **dislocations**:

▶ **sprain** – a complete or partial tearing or stretching of the ligaments around a joint
▶ **dislocation** – a displacement of one or more bone ends at a joint so that their surfaces are no longer in proper contact

4

Mark each of the following statements as either true **(T)** or false **(F)**:

☐ A. A joint is where two or more bones meet.
☐ B. Tissues surrounding the bones of a joint prevent its movement.
☐ C. A sprain occurs when the supporting tissues around a joint are over-stretched or damaged.
☐ D. A dislocation occurs when the bones at a joint are pushed out of their position.

A.T B.F C.T D.T

General signs and symptoms

5

Some or all of the following signs and symptoms occur in most bone and joint injuries –

You may see:

▶ swelling and discolouration

▶ deformity and irregularity

▶ protruding bone ends

▶ inability to use the limb

▶ guarding and tensing of muscles around the injured area

▶ grating noise that can be heard as the bone ends rub together

▶ signs of shock, increasing with severity of the injury

The casualty may complain of:

▶ pain made worse by movement

▶ tenderness on touching

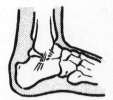
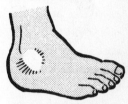

**Sprained ankle
deformity and swelling**

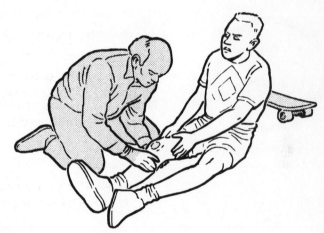

Assess injury

6

Which of the following could indicate a bone or joint injury of the lower limb?

Check ☑ the correct answers:

☐ A. A cut on the lower leg is bleeding profusely.

☐ B. The end of a bone is sticking through the skin of the lower leg.

☐ C. A casualty is pale and sweating. His skin feels cold. His leg is in an unnatural position with the foot turned to the outside.

☐ D. A casualty cannot bend his knee and screams when you touch it.

☐ E. A soccer player has fallen and has a painful, swollen ankle.

B C D E

Principles of first aid

7

The **aims of first aid** for bone and joint injuries are:

▶ to prevent further damage and reduce pain

The first aid principles to be followed are:

◆ perform a scene survey
◆ do a primary survey and give first aid for life-threatening injuries
◆ treat the injury at the incident site
◆ control bleeding from open wounds, if present
◆ if medical help is close by, **steady and support the injured part** in the position of greatest comfort
◆ apply a cold compress, a wrapped, cold pack or ice bag on any closed fracture or injury to reduce pain and control swelling (15 minutes on – 15 minutes off)
◆ apply gentle pressure/compression with a bandage
◆ elevate the injured part, if possible
◆ monitor the casualty closely for any change in his condition
◆ reassure the casualty
◆ do not give anything to eat or drink
◆ give ongoing casualty care until hand over

Note: ◆ All fractures, dislocations and sprains should be immobilized before the casualty is moved, unless the casualty is in immediate danger
◆ Always immobilize in position found

For any closed fracture, sprain or dislocation, keep the casualty as comfortable as possible with:
◆ *R - Rest*
◆ *I - Ice*
◆ *C - Compression/ bandaging*
◆ *E - Elevation*

8

Mark each of the following statements as either true **(T)** or false **(F)**:

☐ A. Cold is applied to all injuries.

☐ B. A fracture of the upper leg is considered to be a minor injury.

☐ C. Displaced bones at joint injuries should be put back in place before immobilizing.

☐ D. If the fracture is open, you should dress the wound before you immobilize the limb.

☐ E. If a fracture is close to a joint, you should immobilize the joint in the position found.

Principles of Immobilization

. . . .

9

Fractured bones and injured joints should be immobilized to prevent further injury and minimize pain.

If medical help is close by, you should:

◆ provide manual support to steady the injured limb until medical help arrives

Manual support

If medical help is delayed or transport is required:

◆ immobilize an injured part to keep it from moving by using:
   ❖ splints
   ❖ slings (for upper limbs)
   ❖ bandages

Splints may be **commercially prepared** or **improvised**. An uninjured body part can also be used as a splint, e.g. a leg, the side of the body.

A good splint should be:

Commercial splints

◆ rigid enough to support the injured limb
◆ long enough:
   ❖ for a fracture between two joints—to extend beyond the joint above and the joint below the fracture site
   ❖ for an injured joint—for the limb to be secured so the joint can't move
◆ wide enough and padded to be comfortable

When immobilization is required, follow these basic guidelines:

◆ don't do anything that causes more pain to the casualty
◆ immobilize the injured area in the position of greatest comfort
◆ check distal circulation before and after immobilization

Improvised splints

. . . .

10

Mark each of the following statements as either true **(T)** or false **(F)**:

☐ A. Healthy body parts are unsuitable as support for broken bones.
☐ B. A splint for a broken lower leg should extend from beyond the heel to above the knee.
☐ C. A hockey stick could be used as a splint.
☐ D. If the ambulance is coming shortly, help the casualty to keep her broken leg still.
☐ E. A broken thigh should be kept aligned and still until the injury has been splinted.

Maintain support

A.F B.T C.T D.T E.T

Objectives

• •

Following the videos and upon completion of your practical skills and this activity book exercise, in an emergency situation you will be able to:

▶ recognize bone and joint injuries

▶ provide first aid for bone and joint injuries of the lower limbs

For further information on bone and joint injuries of the lower limbs, please refer to: *First on the Scene*, the St. John Ambulance first aid and CPR manual, chapter 7, available through your instructor or any major bookstore in your area.

EXERCISE 13

HEAD/SPINAL AND PELVIC INJURIES

Introduction to head/spinal and pelvic injuries

1

A basic knowledge of the structure of **the head, spine** and **pelvis** and **how they relate to each other**, will help you to understand how injury to one part may affect the other part. It will help you to give the appropriate first aid.

Injuries to the head, spine and pelvis are always serious because of the **danger of injury to the nervous system.**

The nervous system is made up of the:

▶ brain

▶ spinal cord

▶ nerves

These delicate tissues are protected by the:

▶ skull

▶ spine

All body functions are controlled by the nervous system. The pelvis is a basin-shaped bony structure connected to the base of the spine.

Nervous system

Skull

Spine

Pelvis

Full skeleton

2

Mark each of the following statements as either true **(T)** or false **(F)**.

☐ A. A blow to the head may cause brain damage.

☐ B. The bony parts of the head and backbone protect the soft parts beneath.

☐ C. The spinal cord and the brain are independent from each other.

☐ D. An injury to the pelvis may involve an injury to the lower part of the spine.

A.T B.T C.F D.T

When to suspect head/spinal injuries

3

The **history/mechanism of injury** is the **first indication** that can lead you to suspect head/spinal injuries.

Head/spinal injuries should be suspected when a casualty:

► has fallen from a height or down the stairs

► has been in a car collision

► has received a blow to the head, spine or pelvis

► has blood or straw-coloured fluid coming from the nose or ears

► is found unconscious and the history is not known

The **injuries** that are commonly **associated** with a **head injury** are **neck and spinal injuries.**

Mechanisms of injury

4

In which of the following circumstances should you suspect that the casualty has suffered head/spinal injuries?

Check ☑ the correct answers.

☐ A. A boy hits his head when he dives into a shallow pool.

☐ B. A young person is found unconscious in bed with an empty bottle of sleeping pills on the floor.

☐ C. A heavy wooden crate falls from a hoist and hits a worker on the back.

☐ D. During a collision, the knees of a person strike the dashboard with great force.

How to recognize head/spinal injuries

5

You can recognize head/spinal injuries by **signs and symptoms.**

You may see:

▶ changes in level of consciousness

▶ unequal size of pupils

▶ loss of movement of any part

▶ unusual lumps on the head or spine

▶ bruising of the head, especially around the eyes and behind the ears

▶ blood or straw-coloured liquid coming from the ears or nose

▶ vomiting

Unequal size of pupils

The casualty may complain of:

▶ severe pain or pressure in the head, neck or back

▶ tingling or loss of feeling or movement in the fingers or toes

▶ nausea

▶ headache

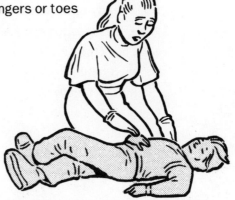

Checking for signs of spinal injuries

6

When you are examining a casualty, which of the following signs and symptoms may indicate head/spinal injuries? Check ☑ the correct answers.

The casualty:

☐ A. Has a big bump on the bony area at the back of the head.

☐ B. Can feel when you squeeze his hand.

☐ C. Can make a fist and wiggle his toes when asked to do so.

☐ D. Tells you of prickling sensations in his hands and feet.

☐ E. Doesn't know what happened and wants to throw up.

☐ F. Has a yellowish fluid dripping from his nose and ears.

Principles of first aid for head/spinal injuries

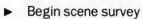

7

When a casualty has head/spinal injuries, **head or neck movement may lead to life-long disability or death.**

Don't move!

I know first aid, can I help you?

► Begin scene survey
► When the **mechanism of injury** suggests possible head/spinal injuries, tell the casualty **NOT TO MOVE**
► Offer to help and obtain consent from the conscious casualty
► **Send** for medical help **immediately**

Are you O.K.?

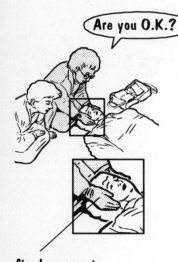

firmly support the head and neck in the position found

> *Advanced medical attention within 1 hour can help avoid permanent damage following spinal injuries*

► **Steady and support** the head and neck in the **position found**
► Assess responsiveness
► Check the airway and for breathing
► If you have a bystander, show him how to steady and support the casualty's head and neck
► If alone, **remind the casualty not to move**
► Continue to perform primary survey
► Give first aid for life-threatening conditions
► Give ongoing casualty care

Continue manual support of the casualty's head and neck in the position found until medical help takes over.

Don't let her head move at all, and if your arms get tired, tell me.

keep elbows firmly supported on thighs or ground

8

Mark each of the following statements as either true (**T**) or false (**F**):

☐ A. A casualty may be hurt for life as a result of damage to the spinal cord and nerves.

☐ B. You should avoid any unnecessary moving of a casualty with suspected head/spinal injuries and obtain medical help promptly.

☐ C. The mechanism of injury is not important for the assessment and first aid for a head/spinal injury.

☐ D. You should caution a conscious person with suspected back injuries to remain as calm as possible.

A.T B.T C.F D.T

9

Maintain an open airway

Your **first aid priority** is maintaining an open airway and breathing.

If the casualty is not breathing:

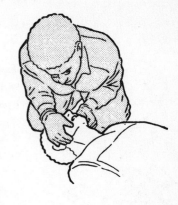

▶ **open** the airway, using the **jaw-thrust without head-tilt,**
this opens the airway without tilting the head and/or moving the neck

▶ give artificial respiration

▶ use your cheek to seal the casualty's nose if
you do not have a mask to ventilate

▶ monitor breathing closely

If the casualty begins to **vomit:**

▶ **turn** the casualty **as a unit** onto the side, keeping
the head and neck in line with the body

▶ **maintain the support for the head and neck** and
quickly clear out the mouth

▶ reposition the casualty, **supporting her head and
neck at all times**

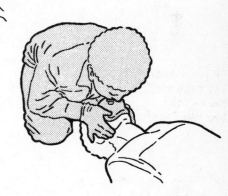

▶ reassess breathing and pulse

▶ resume ventilations if required

▶ give ongoing casualty care until hand over

▶ **continue to support the casualty's head and neck** manually
until medical help takes over

10

Check ☑ the correct completions for the following statements by writing the
appropriate numbers into the squares provided.

When giving artificial respiration to a casualty with a suspected neck injury –

A. The head and neck should:

- ☐ 1. Be tilted backward.
- ☐ 2. Be tilted forward.
- ☐ 3. Not be tilted.

B. When the casualty starts vomiting:

- ☐ 1. Roll the casualty to the side keeping the head and neck in line with the
  body.
- ☐ 2. Turn only the head quickly to the side.
- ☐ 3. Leave the casualty on her back and try to clear the mouth.

A.3   B.1

Bleeding from a scalp wound

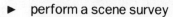
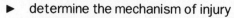

11

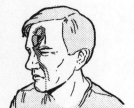

Bleeding from the scalp may be severe even if the wound is superficial. Any scalp wound, depending on the mechanism of injury, could indicate a serious head injury that may cause unconsciousness and breathing problems. If you suspect head/spinal injuries, tell the casualty not to move. If a bystander is available, ask him to steady and support the head and neck in the position found.

To control bleeding from a scalp wound (no head/spinal injury suspected):

- ▶ perform a scene survey
- ▶ determine the mechanism of injury
- ▶ wash hands and put gloves on, if available
- ▶ perform a primary survey and give first aid for life-threatening conditions
- ▶ clean away loose dirt from the wound
- ▶ avoid direct pressure, probing or contaminating the wound
- ▶ apply a thick, sterile dressing large enough to extend well beyond the edges of the wound
- ▶ hold dressing in place with a triangular bandage
- ▶ get medical help promptly
- ▶ give ongoing casualty care until hand over

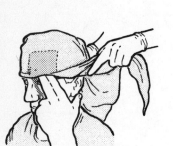

12

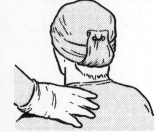

A conscious, breathing casualty is bleeding severely from a scalp wound. Before getting medical help for the casualty, what first aid should you do to control the bleeding?

Check ☑ the correct answers.

- ☐ A. Ask the casualty to maintain gentle pressure on the wound while you bandage.
- ☐ B. Cover the wound with a small adhesive dressing and secure it loosely in place.
- ☐ C. Apply large, soft dressings to the wound and secure them in place with a head bandage.
- ☐ D. Look for hidden dirt inside the wound and pick it out with your fingers.

Bandaging a scalp wound

A C

Bump on the head

13

A bump on the head is a very common injury, especially in children. It may be harmless. However, as any head injury, it should be taken seriously because of the possibility of injury to the brain.

To give first aid, for a bump on the head:

▶ be guided by the mechanism of injury

▶ if you suspect head/spinal injuries, tell the casualty not to move

▶ if you don't suspect head/spinal injuries, keep the casualty at rest

▶ put a cold compress or ice bag (15 minutes on – 15 minutes off) on the bruise to relieve pain and control swelling

▶ check the casualty often for:

   ■ loss of consciousness (ask him questions, e.g. what his name is, where he lives)

   ■ a change in breathing, pulse and skin temperature

   ■ headache, nausea or vomiting

   ■ blood or straw-coloured fluid coming from the ears or nose

   ■ seizures

▶ if you see any of these signs or symptoms developing, even after many days, get medical help immediately

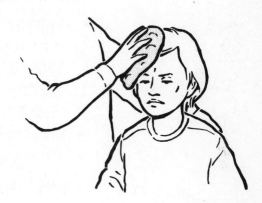

14

Mark each of the following statements as either true **(T)** or false **(F)**.

☐ A. A person who has hit his head could have injured his brain.

☐ B. A person who is confused after a fall on the head should be observed carefully.

☐ C. You should apply heat to the bruised area.

☐ D. If the casualty's breathing becomes slow and laboured, you should get medical attention immediately.

☐ E. Any discharge from the ears could be a sign of a serious head injury.

> ⚠ **Warning!**
>
> Any casualty who has lost consciousness for a few minutes should be taken to medical help. Follow medical advice on what signs and symptoms to watch for as possible indicators of a head injury.

A.T B.T C.F D.T E.T

Bleeding from the ear

15

Bleeding from the ear can have different causes. Bleeding, accompanied by a straw-coloured fluid, may indicate a fracture of the skull. To give the appropriate first aid, you have to **establish the mechanism of injury**.

If head/spinal injuries are not suspected:

▶ perform a scene survey
▶ perform a primary survey and give first aid for life-threatening conditions
▶ check for the cause of bleeding
▶ secure a dressing loosely over the ear
▶ place the conscious casualty semisitting, inclined toward the injured side
▶ place the unconscious casualty into the recovery position on the injured side
▶ obtain medical help
▶ give ongoing casualty care until hand over

Applying dressing

Positioning

If head/spinal injuries are suspected:

▶ perform a scene survey
▶ tell the casualty **not to move**. If a bystander is available, ask him to **steady and support the head and neck in the position found**
▶ do a primary survey and give first aid for life-threatening conditions
▶ make no attempt to stop the flow of blood or other fluids
▶ do not pack the ear with gauze
▶ place a dressing loosely over the ear
▶ check breathing frequently
▶ obtain medical help immediately
▶ give ongoing casualty care until medical help takes over

Don't move!

firmly support the head and neck in the position found and apply dressing

16

From the following statements, check the correct choices for giving first aid when blood is oozing from a conscious casualty's ear.

When head/spinal injuries are suspected:

☐ A. Ask the casualty to stay completely still in the position found.
☐ B. Tape gauze dressings lightly over the ear.
☐ C. Support the casualty in a semisitting position.

When no head/spinal injuries are suspected:

☐ D. Tape gauze dressings lightly over the ear.
☐ E. Place the casualty into the recovery position.

A B D

Head/spinal injuries—review

17

1. Which of the following illustration show a mechanism of injury that would indicate possible head/spinal injuries? Check ☑ your answers.

   ☐ A.

   ☐ B.

   ☐ C.

   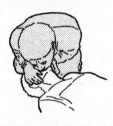

   ☐ D.

2. If you suspect head/spinal injuries, which of the following illustrations shows the right way to open the airway? Check ☑ your answer.

   ☐ A. Jaw-thrust without head-tilt   ☐ B. Head-tilt chin-lift

3. Which of the following illustrations shows the best positioning for a casualty with head/spinal injuries? Check ☑ your answer.

   ☐ A.

   ☐ B.

1.B 1.C 2.A 3.B

When to suspect a pelvic injury

18

A **pelvic injury** is any break or crack in the bones of the pelvis.

When arriving at an emergency scene, look for the causes and the history of the incident. Try to find out what happened to the casualty's body and how much force was involved.

The mechanism of injury for a pelvic injury is usually:

▶ **direct force,** e.g. a direct crush or heavy impact and may involve injury to the organs in the pelvic area, especially the bladder

▶ **indirect force,** e.g. in a fall, the force is applied to the pelvis through the legs or hip joints, or by pulling or twisting

In the elderly, even a simple fall may cause a fracture in the pelvic area.

Mechanisms of injury

19

Mark each of the following statements as either true **(T)** or false **(F)**.

☐ A. To suffer a broken pelvis, a person must receive a blow right on the pelvic bones.

☐ B. A violent crushing of the knees against the dashboard in a car collision can result in a pelvic fracture.

☐ C. The pelvis is a strong, thick structure which is rarely injured in people over 60 years of age.

☐ D. A construction worker who has fallen from a ladder and landed on his feet may have injured his pelvis.

A.F B.T C.F D.T

Signs and symptoms of a pelvic injury

. . . .

20

If the pelvis has been injured –

You may see:

▶ signs of shock (internal bleeding may be present)

▶ inability of the casualty to stand or walk

▶ inability to urinate or a bloody urine

The casualty may complain of:

▶ sharp pain in the hips, groin and the small of the back

▶ increased pain when moving

▶ urge to urinate

An injury of the pelvis may result in damage to the **lower spine** or to the **bladder,** leading to serious infection.

Check for shock

If you suspect a pelvic injury, do not squeeze the hips together.

Check abdomen

Check lower back

Check pelvis

. . . .

21

Of the following statements, check ☑ the conditions of a casualty which may indicate a pelvic fracture.

☐ A. Strong discomfort around the pelvic area.

☐ B. The passing of pinkish urine.

☐ C. Pallor, sweating and a rapid pulse.

☐ D. Deformity of the feet.

☐ E. Moving around freely.

Principles of first aid for a pelvic injury

22

A **pelvic injury** is often **associated with a spinal injury** and should be treated with the same care as a spinal injury:

▶ begin scene survey

▶ when the mechanism of injury suggests a pelvic injury, tell the casualty **NOT TO MOVE**

▶ offer to help and obtain consent from the conscious casualty

▶ send for medical help immediately

▶ steady and support the casualty in the position found

▶ assess responsiveness

▶ check the airway and for breathing

▶ if there is a bystander, show him how to steady and support the casualty

▶ if alone, remind casualty not to move

▶ continue with the primary survey

▶ give first aid for any life-threatening condition

▶ **support both sides of the pelvis with padded objects to prevent movement**, e.g. rolled blankets

▶ give ongoing casualty care

Continue to support the casualty manually until medical help takes over.

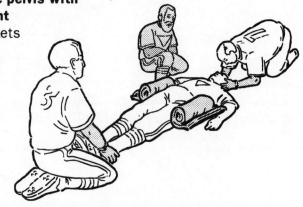

23

The mechanism of injury and the signs and symptoms indicate that the casualty is suffering from an injured pelvis. Medical help has been called and will arrive soon. What first aid should you give in the meantime?

Check ☑ the correct answers.

☐ A. Place the casualty in the recovery position.

☐ B. Tell the casualty to remain as still as possible.

☐ C. Place a rolled blanket on each side of the pelvis to keep the casualty from moving sideways and causing more pain.

☐ D. Reassure the casualty, maintain body heat and keep the casualty from moving until the ambulance arrives.

First aid for pelvic injuries—review

24

A baseball player was hit with a baseball bat in his lower back. He complains about sharp pain in the hips and in the small of the back. There are several bystanders ready to help.

Based on the history and mechanism of injury, number the correct first aid procedures for this casualty, **in the order you should perform them,** by placing the appropriate numbers into the squares provided.

☐ A. Take charge.

☐ B. Support the pelvis.

Don't move!
Can I help?

Get medical help.

☐ C. Check the airway.

☐ D. Check breathing.

☐ E. Steady and support head and neck.

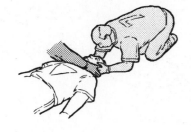

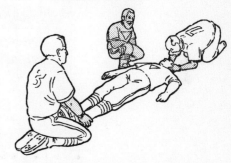

☐ F. Do a rapid body survey.

☐ G. Check for shock.

☐ H. Give ongoing casualty care.

A.1 B.7 C.3 D.4 E.2 F.6 G.5 H.8

Objectives

· ·

Upon completion of this activity book exercise, in an emergency situation, you will be able to:

▶ recognize head/spinal injuries

▶ provide first aid for suspected head/spinal injuries

▶ control bleeding from the scalp and ear

▶ recognize a pelvic injury

▶ provide first aid for a suspected pelvic injury

For further information on head/spinal and pelvic injuries, please refer to:
First on the Scene, the St. John Ambulance first aid and CPR manual, chapter 7, available through your instructor or any major bookstore in your area.

CHEST INJURIES

8 min

Introduction to chest injuries

1

A basic knowledge of the structures of the chest will help you to give first aid for injuries in this area. The **chest cavity** is formed by the:

► breastbone (sternum)

► ribs

► spine

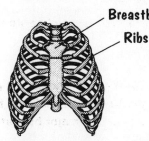

Chest cavity

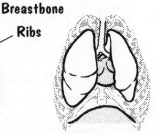

Breastbone

Ribs

Chest cavity, inside view

These bones protect the **lungs**, **heart** and **major blood vessels.**
The chest cavity is separated from the abdominal cavity by the **diaphragm.**

There are two general types of chest injuries:

► **closed** – the skin remains unbroken (usually caused by a blunt force)

► **open** – the skin is broken (when the chest is punctured)

Chest injuries **can be life-threatening** because of the possibility of –

► severe breathing problems

► damage to the heart and lungs

► internal bleeding

Blunt force

Knife wound

2

Mark each of the following statements as either true **(T)** or false **(F)**.

☐ A. The lungs and the heart are located in the abdominal cavity.

☐ B. The breastbone, ribs and spine form the chest cavity.

☐ C. Wounds to the chest seldom cause serious problems.

☐ D. Laboured breathing may be seen with any chest injury.

☐ E. Broken ribs can cause injury to the structures inside the chest.

A.F B.T C.F D.T E.T

Penetrating chest wound

· ·

3

A penetrating or "sucking" chest wound occurs when an object punctures the chest. Through the open chest wound **air enters** directly into the chest cavity causing serious breathing problems.

Some or all of the following signs and symptoms may be present –

You may observe:

▶ sounds of air being sucked into the chest when the casualty breathes in

▶ blood-stained bubbles at the wound site when the casualty breathes out

▶ coughing up of frothy blood

▶ inability to expand one or both sides of the chest

▶ laboured breathing

▶ signs of shock

The casualty may complain of:

▶ pain during breathing

A penetrating chest wound **can be life-threatening**. The aim of first aid is to restore effective breathing immediately.

Gunshot wound

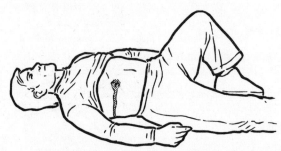

Penetrating chest wound with blood-stained bubbles

· ·

4

By which of the following signs and symptoms would you recognize a penetrating chest wound?

Check ☑ the correct answers.

☐ A. The casualty moans with pain when breathing.

☐ B. Foamy blood appears around the wound.

☐ C. Breathing is very quiet.

☐ D. Clear fluid is seen coming from the mouth.

☐ E. The casualty's skin is cool and clammy and the pulse is fast and weak.

First aid for a penetrating chest wound—review

. . . .

5

You have seen the video and practised the first aid procedures for a penetrating chest wound.

Place the steps below into **the correct order of performance**. Write the appropriate numbers into the boxes.

☐ **A.** Check circulation (shock) and perform a rapid body survey.

☐ **B.** Cover the wound with the casualty's hand.

☐ **C.** Give ongoing casualty care. Check the dressing frequently to ensure air can escape.

☐ **D.** Position the casualty. Cover the wound with a dressing and tape on three sides.

☐ **E.** Expose the wound.

☐ **F.** Check breathing.

A.4 B.2 C.6 D.5 E.1 F.3

Flail chest

. . . .

6

A **flail chest** results when several ribs in the same area are broken in more than one place. The **mechanism of injury** may be a severe blow or a crushing force to the chest, e.g. a car crash, a fall or being struck by a large object.

A flail chest may be recognized by the following –

You may see:

▶ abnormal movement of the injured part of the chest wall during breathing

▶ laboured, ineffective breathing

The casualty may complain of:

▶ pain during breathing

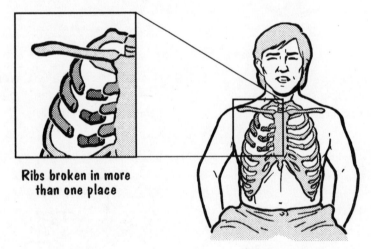

Ribs broken in more than one place

Flail chest

. . . .

7

Mark each of the following statements as either true **(T)** or false **(F)**.

☐ A. A flail chest can happen when a person is thrown against the steering wheel.

☐ B. When many ribs are broken in several places, a part of the chest does not rise and fall with the rest of the rib cage.

☐ C. A flail chest does not affect the casualty's breathing.

☐ D. A flail chest results when an object punctures the chest from the outside.

First aid for a flail chest

8

The force that caused a flail chest may have also caused head/spinal injuries.

As soon as you suspect major injuries, give first aid as for a casualty with suspected head/spinal injuries:

- ▶ tell the casualty not to move
- ▶ obtain medical help
- ▶ leave the casualty in the position found and support the head and neck
- ▶ perform a primary survey, check airway and breathing
- ▶ if the casualty complains of difficulty breathing and pain in the chest, expose and examine the injury. Hand support over the injury may make breathing easier
- ▶ do not apply padding over the area or wrap bandages around the chest
- ▶ give first aid for ineffective breathing if needed
- ▶ continue your primary survey, check circulation
- ▶ give ongoing casualty care until medical help takes over

9

A conscious casualty of a head-on collision has difficulties breathing and shows signs and symptoms of a flail chest. An ambulance has been called. What first aid should you give until medical help takes over?

Check ☑ the correct answers.

- ☐ A. Ensure that the casualty is not moving.

- ☐ B. Check breathing and help the casualty to breathe if required.

- ☐ C. Bandage a firm pad over the flail area.

- ☐ D. Place the casualty into a semisitting position.

A   B

Closed fracture of the rib cage

10

Guarding

Closed fractures of one or more ribs may show no signs of external injury and are not usually life-threatening. The mechanism of injury is commonly a direct blow to the chest.

You may observe:

◆ shallow, uncoordinated breathing

◆ bruising or deformity at the suspected fracture site

◆ guarded movement

◆ grating sound on movement

◆ if lungs are punctured by the broken ribs, casualty may cough up frothy blood and have increased difficulty breathing

The casualty may complain of:

◆ pain at the fracture site that increases with movement

To give first aid, you should:

◆ perform a scene survey

◆ perform a primary survey

◆ expose and examine the injury site if the casualty has difficulty breathing. Hand support over the injured area may make breathing easier

◆ place the conscious casualty in a semisitting position, inclined toward the injured side to help breathing

◆ support the arm on the injured side in a St. John tubular sling. This will transfer the weight of the arm to the uninjured side

◆ obtain medical help

◆ give ongoing casualty care until hand over to medical help

Note: If the casualty shows severe breathing difficulties and signs of shock, give first aid as for a flail chest

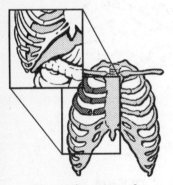

**Closed fracture of
the rib cage**

Positioning

11

Mark each of the following statements as either true (**T**) or false (**F**).

☐ A. To relieve the pain when breathing, ask the casualty to press with the hand against the site of the injury.

☐ B. Bandage a pillow tightly over the injury site.

☐ C. Apply a sling to support the arm on the injured side and reduce its weight.

☐ D. If the casualty tells you that he has more pain after you applied the sling, remove it.

Blast injury

. . . .

11

The violent shock waves from an explosion can seriously damage the lungs and internal organs. Even when there is no sign of other injury, a life-threatening breathing emergency can result from a blast injury.

To assess a blast injury, consider:

▶ the mechanism of injury (type and extent of explosion, casualty's closeness to the explosion)
▶ the signs and symptoms of the casualty

You may see:

▶ frothy blood being coughed up
▶ laboured breathing
▶ signs of shock

The casualty may complain of:

▶ chest pain

To give first aid for a blast injury:

▶ perform a scene survey
▶ if the casualty is unconscious, get medical help immediately
▶ perform a primary survey and give first aid for life-threatening injuries
▶ give assisted breathing, if required
▶ assist the conscious casualty to a semisitting position to ease breathing
▶ place the unconscious casualty into the recovery position
▶ give ongoing casualty care until medical help takes over

Wave of explosion

. . . .

12

Mark each of the following statements as either true **(T)** or false **(F)**.

☐ A. It is important to know how close the casualty was to an explosion.
☐ B. A conscious casualty with a blast injury should be put into the recovery position.
☐ C. If a casualty who has been injured in a gas explosion, has bubbly blood coming from the mouth, he needs immediate medical help.
☐ D. If there are no signs of bleeding or fractures, blast injuries are not serious.

A.T B.F C.T D.F

Objectives

• •

Following the video and upon completion of your practical skills and this activity book exercise, in an emergency situation, you will be able to:

▶ recognize a chest injury

▶ recognize a penetrating chest wound

▶ provide first aid for a penetrating chest wound

▶ recognize a flail chest

▶ provide first aid for a flail chest

▶ recognize a rib fracture and provide first aid

▶ recognize a blast injury to the chest and provide first aid

For further information on chest injuries, please refer to:
First on the Scene, the St. John Ambulance first aid and CPR manual, chapters 3 and 7, available through your instructor or any major bookstore in your area.

WOUND CARE

10 min

Wounds

· ·

1

A **wound** is any break in the **soft tissues** of the body.

A wound can be either open or closed:

▶ **open wound** – there is a break in the outer layer of the skin. It results in bleeding and may permit the entrance of germs that cause infection

▶ **closed wound** – there is no break in the outer layer of the skin. There is no external bleeding and little risk of infection. Soft tissue damage occurs under the skin, e.g. a bruise.

The aims in the care of wounds are to:

▶ stop bleeding

▶ prevent further contamination and infection

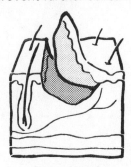

Open wound

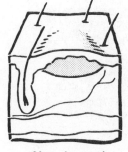

Closed wound

· ·

2

Mark each of the following statements as either true **(T)** or false **(F)**.

☐ A. Loss of blood usually occurs when there is a break in the skin.

☐ B. A wound is any injury in which just the skin is punctured.

☐ C. A deep cut in the finger is an example of an open wound.

☐ D. An open wound should be kept clean to prevent complications.

A.T B.F C.T D.T

Contamination and infection

. . . .

3

Contamination (germs, dirt or foreign material) in an open wound may lead to **infection**. All open wounds are contaminated to some degree.

Prevent further contamination of an open wound. Follow these steps for cleansing a minor wound:

▶ wash your hands with soap and water or use clean gloves, if possible, before giving first aid

▶ do not cough or breathe directly over the wound

▶ do not touch the wound

▶ gently wash the wound under slowly running water if there is loose material on the surface

▶ protect the wound with a temporary, preferably sterile or clean, dressing

▶ wash surrounding skin with clean swabs. Wipe away from the wound

▶ dry surrounding skin with clean swabs. Wipe away from the wound

▶ remove temporary dressing

▶ cover the wound promptly with a sterile or clean dressing and tape in place

▶ remove and dispose of gloves when wound care is completed

▶ wash your hands and any other skin area that has been in contact with the casualty's blood

Clean a wound

Cover a wound

Remove gloves

. . . .

4

Which of the following actions are good first aid procedures to prevent further contamination of an open wound?

Check ☑ the correct answers.

☐ A. Blow loose dirt away from a wound.

☐ B. Use your fingers to remove visible dirt from a wound.

☐ C. Use soap and water to clean your hands before applying dressings.

☐ D. Brush off both sides of the dressing to ensure it is clean before you apply it.

☐ E. Wipe away from the wound with a piece of gauze to remove dirt.

☐ F. Protect the wound with a clean dressing.

C E F

Tetanus infection

· ·

5

Any open wound can be contaminated with a bacillus (germ) that causes **tetanus (lockjaw)**.

Tetanus is a serious disease that can be fatal. It is characterized by muscle spasms and stiffness of the jaw. The tetanus germ is found in soil, dust and animal feces. Particular care should be taken with wounds caused by farming or gardening tools and rusty nails. Careful washing can flush away the bacillus before it can cause infection in minor wounds. The tetanus germs thrive only in deep wounds.

As a first aider, **it is your duty to advise any casualty with an open wound to protect himself against tetanus** by seeing a doctor as soon as possible.

A person can be protected against tetanus by immunization.

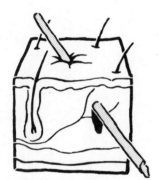

Puncture wound

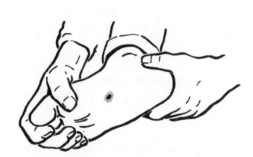

Puncture wound on sole of foot

· ·

6

Mark each of the following statements as either true **(T)** or false **(F)**.

☐ A. Tetanus infection is a threat only if a wound is caused by rusty metal.

☐ B. The tetanus germ grows best in deep wounds.

☐ C. The tetanus germ can infect the body through the food we eat.

☐ D. The disease, also called lockjaw, can result in death.

☐ E. Deep wounds with dirt inside should be checked by a doctor following first aid.

A.F B.T C.F D.T E.T

Dressing, bandages and slings

Improvised dressings

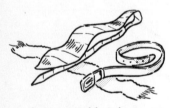

Commercial dressings

Commercial bandages

Improvised bandages

7

Dressings and **bandages** are basic tools of first aid.

A dressing is a protective covering placed on a wound to help control bleeding, to absorb blood from a wound and to prevent further contamination and infection.

Dressings and bandages can be **commercially prepared** or **improvised**.

A dressing should be:

► sterile or as clean as possible
► highly absorbent to keep the wound dry
► thick, soft and compressible so that pressure can be applied evenly over the affected area
► non-stick and lint-free to reduce the possibility of sticking to the wound
  ▪ gauze, cotton or linen make good dressings
► large enough to completely cover the wound

A bandage is a material used to:

► hold dressings in place
► maintain pressure over a wound
► support a limb or joint
► immobilize parts of the body
► secure a splint

The **triangular bandage** is the most versatile bandage and may also be used as a:

► ring pad
► arm sling
► St. John tubular sling

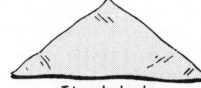

Triangular bandage

Broad bandage

8

Several choices for improvised dressings and bandages are described below.

Check ☑ the ones you could safely use.

☐ A. A piece of clean bed linen large enough to cover a wound.
☐ B. A cotton towel cut to size to extend over the edges of a wound.
☐ C. Fluffy cotton balls make a good covering for a wound.
☐ D. A belt can be used as an improvised sling.
☐ E.. A large garbage bag can be made into a sling.

Arm sling

A B D E

Bleeding from the nose

. . . .

9

A nosebleed may occur spontaneously or may be caused by:

▶ blowing the nose

▶ injury to the nose or skull

To control a nosebleed, you should:

▶ do a scene survey

▶ do a primary survey

▶ place the casualty in a sitting position with the head slightly forward

▶ tell the casualty to **pinch the soft parts of the nose firmly** with the thumb and forefinger for **about 10 minutes** or until bleeding stops

▶ loosen tight clothing around the casualty's neck and chest

▶ keep the casualty quiet to avoid increased bleeding

▶ get medical help if bleeding does not stop or if bleeding recurs

▶ when bleeding stops, tell the casualty **not to blow his nose** for a few hours

Do not try to stop a nosebleed caused by a head injury!

If the mechanism of injury indicates a possible head injury, you should:

▶ steady and support the head and neck

▶ wipe away the external trickling blood—do not try to stop it and do not poke the nostrils with tissues

▶ call for medical help immediately

. . . .

10

From the statements below, check ☑ the correct first aid procedures for a nosebleed.

☐ A. Send for medical help before you start first aid.

☐ B. Sit the person down and tilt his head back.

☐ C. Ask the person to press on the soft parts of his nose until there is no blood flow.

☐ D. If blood dribbles from the nose after a casualty was involved in a car crash, don't try to stop it. Get an ambulance right away.

C D

Bleeding from the gums, tongue and cheek

Bleeding tongue

Bleeding cheek

A bleeding gum should be treated as a sign of a boken jaw until proven otherwise

11

Bleeding from the gums, tongue or cheek can occur following a tooth extraction, a knocked out tooth or other injury and can be very heavy.

There is a danger of the blood entering the airway causing choking, or the stomach causing nausea:

◆ **always ensure an open airway**

Give first aid for bleeding from the gums as follows:

◆ wash hands and put gloves on
◆ place a gauze pad firmly on the tooth socket or injury site. Use a pad thick enough to keep the teeth apart when biting
◆ ask the casualty to bite on the pad until the bleeding stops and to support the chin with his hands, if possible
◆ obtain medical or dental advice if bleeding cannot be controlled
◆ do not wash out the mouth after bleeding has stopped. It may disturb clots and cause bleeding to resume

If a tooth has been knocked out, do not touch the roots. Gently place it in a cup of milk and see a dentist immediately. If milk is not available, the tooth may be preserved in a saline solution or wrapped in plastic wrap kept moist with the casualty's saliva.

Give first aid for bleeding from the tongue and cheek as follows:

◆ wash hands and put on gloves
◆ use a sterile dressing or clean cloth and compress the bleeding part between the finger and thumb until the bleeding stops

Knocked out tooth

12

Mark each of the following statements as either true **(T)** or false **(F)**.

▢ A. Severe bleeding inside the mouth will usually stop on its own.
▢ B. Bleeding from the mouth could be a potentially life-threatening emergency.
▢ C. Vomiting may follow a mouth injury.
▢ D. Pressure will usually stop bleeding from the tongue.
▢ E. The roots of a knocked out tooth should be cleaned thoroughly.

A.F B.T C.T D.T E.F

Abdominal injuries

. . . .

13

The **abdomen** is the body area below the chest.

The **abdominal cavity** is the space between the diaphragm and the lower part of the pelvis. This cavity contains the abdominal organs, e.g. stomach, liver, spleen.

An injury to the abdomen may be a **closed wound** or an **open wound.**

Closed wounds are those in which the abdomen is injured but the skin remains unbroken. The mechanism of injury could be, e.g. a severe blow or a crush injury.

Open wounds are those in which the skin is broken. The mechanism of injury could be, e.g. a puncture wound or a cut with a knife.

Closed and open wounds of the abdomen may result in injuries to the internal organs.

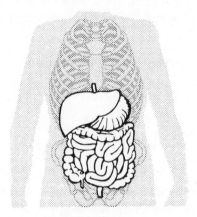

The abdomen

. . . .

14

Mark each of the following statements as either true **(T)** or false **(F)**.

☐ A. Many internal organs are located in the lower body cavity.

☐ B. An abdominal injury without obvious bleeding does not need any first aid.

☐ C. A gunshot wound of the abdomen is a closed wound.

☐ D. An open or closed wound of the abdomen may cause damage to the underlying tissues.

☐ E. A deep, open wound to the abdomen may cause external and internal bleeding.

A.T B.F C.F D.T E.T

First aid for abdominal wounds

15

Semisitting

Apply dressing

Tape dressing

Any abdominal wound should be treated as a serious condition because there is a danger of:

▶ **severe internal bleeding** from damaged organs

▶ **contamination** from the contents of the ruptured organs

This may lead to:

▶ **severe shock**

▶ **infection**

An open abdominal wound may allow internal organs to protrude.

To give first aid for an open abdominal wound:

▶ consider the history and mechanism of injury

▶ prevent the wound from opening wider by positioning the casualty with head and shoulders slightly raised and supported, and knees raised

Internal organs not protruding:

▶ apply a dry dressing

▶ bandage firmly over the dressing

▶ give nothing by mouth

▶ obtain medical help immediately

16

From the choices below, check ☑ the correct first aid procedures for a conscious casualty with an abdominal wound when organs are not protruding:

☐ A. Position the casualty so that the wound stays closed.

☐ B. If the casualty complains of thirst, give sips of water.

☐ C. Cover the wound with a dry gauze dressing and bandage securely.

☐ D. If the casualty starts to vomit, place him into the recovery position.

A C

17

Internal organs protruding:

▶ do not replace organs

▶ apply a large, moist, sterile dressing to prevent drying of the organs

▶ secure dressings without pressure

▶ give nothing by mouth

▶ obtain medical help immediately

▶ if the casualty is coughing or vomiting, support the abdomen with two broad bandages

▶ give ongoing casualty care until medical help takes over

Expose area

Semisitting

Place moist dressings

Tape dressings in place

Apply broad bandages

18

From the choices below, check ☑ the correct first aid procedures for a conscious casualty with an abdominal wound when organs are protruding.

☐ A. Gently push the organs back into the abdomen.

☐ B. Cover the wound with a clean, damp cloth and bandage lightly.

☐ C. Give nothing to eat or drink.

☐ D. If the casualty starts to vomit, apply more bandages to prevent further opening of the wound.

B C D

Objectives

· ·

Following the video and upon completion of your practical skills and this activity book exercise, in an emergency situation, you will be able to:

▶ take measures to prevent further contamination and infection of wounds

▶ use dressings, bandages and slings in first aid procedures

▶ control external bleeding from a wound with an embedded object

▶ control bleeding from the nose, gums, tongue and cheek

▶ provide first aid for a wound in the palm of the hand

▶ recognize an abdominal wound

▶ provide first aid for an abdominal wound

For further information on chest injuries, please refer to:
First on the Scene, the St. John Ambulance first aid and CPR manual, chapter 6, available through your instructor or any major bookstore in your area.

EXERCISE 16

MULTIPLE CASUALTY MANAGEMENT

Triage

1

When the number of **casualties is greater than the number of first aiders**, you must decide in which order the injured should get **first aid**, and which casualties should be taken to **medical help** first. This process of decision making is called triage.

Triage is the process of sorting and classifying casualties by assigning **priorities** of **first aid** and **transportation** for all the injured.

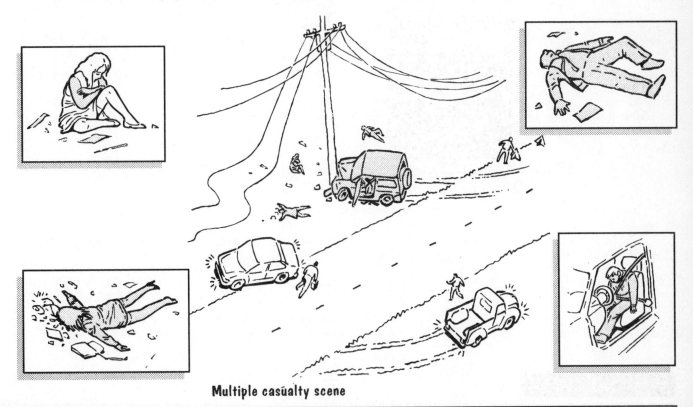

Multiple casualty scene

· ·

1   (cont'd)

If you are alone, perform the scene survey and a complete primary survey, including first aid for immediate life-threatening problems, in turn on all casualties.

The mechanism of injury will help you decide to which casualty you should go first.

Ensure the following:

A – An open airway; with support of head and neck, if head/spinal injuries are suspected

B – Breathing, to allow for adequate ventilation

C – Circulation, including control of severe bleeding and first aid for shock

Remember, each casualty should be examined and given first aid for these life-threatening conditions before any other injuries are cared for.

Severe bleeding

Obviously dead

Head injuries

Stopped breathing

· ·

2

Mark each of the following statements as either true **(T)** or false **(F)**.

☐ A. Triage should be used at any multiple casualty situation where you will not be able to give first aid to everyone at once.

☐ B. In triage, the first aider may have to decide which casualty receives attention first.

☐ C. If you arrive at an emergency scene alone and there are three casualties, you need to establish priorities for giving first aid.

☐ D. In triage, only priorities of transportation are decided.

A.T B.T C.T D.F

Priorities

• •

3

The **sorting and assigning of priorities** should be done as soon as you can do so safely. Casualties are usually sorted into **three levels** according to their priorities of emergency care.

Highest priority—those casualties requiring immediate first aid and transportation because of:

▶ airway and breathing difficulties

▶ cardiac arrest, if sufficient first aiders are available to give first aid for other life-threatening conditions

▶ severe bleeding

▶ shock

▶ severe head injuries

▶ severe burns

▶ severe medical problems, e.g. poisoning, diabetes and cardiovascular emergencies

▶ open chest or abdominal wounds

Second priority—those casualties who probably can wait one-hour for medical help without risk to their lives:

▶ burns

▶ major or multiple fractures

▶ back injuries (with or without spinal damage)

Lowest priority—those casualties who may receive first aid and transportation last:

▶ minor fractures

▶ minor bleeding

▶ behavioural problems

▶ cardiac arrest, if enough first aiders are not available to care for other casualties

▶ obviously dead

• •

4

An industrial explosion has caused serious injuries to four workers. Following the scene survey, you note that all are conscious. One worker is bleeding profusely. Another worker has painful burns on his arms. The third is pale, sweating and showing signs of shock, and the fourth seems hysterical.

If alone, in which order would you give first aid to these casualties? Place the appropriate number into the boxes.

☐ A. The worker who is burned.

☐ B. The worker who is bleeding profusely.

☐ C. The worker who is in shock.

☐ D. The worker who is walking around screaming.

B.1 C.2 A.3 D.4

5

Your ability to save lives depends on your knowledge and skills to evaluate which casualties need immediate first aid and which casualties can wait without being harmed further. Trust your own judgement and do what is best for most casualties.

Procedures to follow:

▶ if there **is more than one first aider** at the scene, the most knowledgeable first aider should take charge and do the triage

▶ complete a primary survey on all casualties first and give first aid for immediate life-threatening problems

▶ call for additional assistance if needed

▶ assign available first aiders and equipment to the highest priority casualties

▶ transport the highest priority casualties and those that are stabilized first

▶ reassess casualties regularly for changes in condition

When you are caring for one or more casualties, remember that:

▶ **assigned priorities for giving first aid and transportation should be reviewed often. They should be changed if any of the casualties' conditions require more urgent care.**

6

You are applying direct pressure to a severely bleeding wound of the conscious casualty's leg. Suddenly another casualty starts gasping for air and stops breathing. What should you do?

From the following options, check ☑ the correct answer.

☐ A. Continue giving first aid to the bleeding casualty.

☐ B. Show the bleeding casualty how to keep pressure on his wound and immediately give first aid to the casualty who stopped breathing.

☐ C. Call out for help and wait for a bystander who could assist you.

☐ D. Bandage the bleeding wound to maintain pressure and elevate the arm in a sling before you give first aid to the non-breathing casualty.

Lightning injuries

7

Casualties who **have no pulse** are normally assigned the lowest priority, unless there are enough first aiders available to give first aid to all casualties.

Lightning injuries are an exception to this rule—**reverse usual triage procedures:**

▶ if someone has been struck by lightning, give first aid for the **apparently dead first**. Casualties of a lightning strike have a greater chance of being revived than a casualty whose heart has stopped because of other causes

Follow these steps

▶ Perform a scene survey and make the area safe, e.g. broken trees, glass

Note: Persons who are struck by lightning are safe to handle. There is no danger of being electrocuted by touching them.

▶ Get a brief history and establish the mechanism of injury

▶ Steady and support the casualty's head and neck to prevent a possible spinal injury from becoming worse

▶ Perform a primary survey

▶ Begin AR and CPR to maintain breathing and circulation

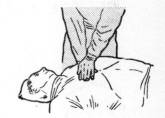

The key to survival is an early, vigorous and prolonged resuscitation effort

▶ Once breathing and the heartbeat are restored, monitor breathing and pulse continuously. The casualties may arrest again

▶ Give ongoing casualty care until hand over to medical help

8

Mark each of the following statements as either true **(T)** or false **(F)**.

☐ A. When a person has been hit by lightning, his heart may stop beating.

☐ B. During triage for lightning injuries, a person who is not breathing and has no pulse should always be given the lowest priority.

☐ C. You should continue resuscitation for a casualty of a lightning strike, even if the casualty appears lifeless.

☐ D. The person whose heart has stopped due to a lightning strike is more likely to survive than other casualties.

A.T B.F C.T D.T

Objectives

• •

Following the videos and upon completion of your practical skills and this activity book exercise, in an emergency situation, you will be able to:

▶ establish priorities of first aid and transportation in a multiple casualty situation

▶ provide emergency care for multiple casualties according to changing first aid priorities

▶ provide ongoing casualty care for multiple casualties

For further information on multiple casualty management, please refer to:
First on the Scene, the St. John Ambulance first aid and CPR manual, chapter 1, available through your instructor or any major bookstore in your area.

EXERCISE 17

RESCUE CARRIES

8 min

Principles of safety for moving a casualty

1

In most emergency situations, **do not move a casualty**, except for reasons of safety. Moving a casualty poses dangers to the first aider as well as to the casualty. However, there are times when you have to move a casualty **for safety or essential life-saving first aid.**

Before you try to move an injured person, consider the following **principles of safety:**

▶ select the method that will pose the least risk to yourself and the casualty

▶ you can be of little help to a casualty if you injure yourself in the rescue

▶ only try to move a casualty you are sure you can safely handle

▶ **support and immobilization** of the injuries should be provided before and during the move

▶ move a casualty the shortest possible distance

▶ use as many bystanders as you need to keep risks to a minimum

Ensure safety
at the scene

2

In which of the following situations should you try to move a casualty before giving first aid?

Check ☑ the correct answers.

- [ ] A. A mechanic is lying inside a burning car.
- [ ] B. An elderly man is found unconscious on the sidewalk.
- [ ] C. A woman is lying in a ditch of water with her face submerged.
- [ ] D. A teenager is lying at the foot of a long stairway.
- [ ] E. A child is floating on the lake under an overturned boat.

A C E

Lifting techniques

3

When lifting and transporting heavy objects, such as a casualty, protect yourself from injury. Rescuers often suffer muscle strain caused by using incorrect body mechanics when lifting and moving a casualty.

You should use proper body mechanics:

When lifting –

- ▶ stand close to the casualty
- ▶ bend your knees; do not stoop
- ▶ get a good grip on the casualty or equipment
- ▶ lift, using the thigh, leg and abdominal muscles, and keeping your back straight
- ▶ when turning, follow your feet, do not twist your body

Ensure that rescuers lift together on a signal.

When lowering –

- ▶ reverse the procedure
- ▶ remember that poor body mechanics can exert extreme pressure on the lower back and may cause muscle and disc injuries

If the rescuers are unskilled, practise the proper techniques before moving the casualty.

4

Which of the following are safety practices that would protect first aiders and the casualty during a rescue procedure?

Check ☑ the correct answers.

- ☐ A. Keep your legs straight as you bend from the waist to lift the casualty with your arms.
- ☐ B. Use the power of your legs as you lift a casualty.
- ☐ C. Make sure that all rescuers can perform the procedure safely before lifting a casualty.
- ☐ D. Immobilize the casualty's injuries to prevent them from becoming worse.

B   C   D

One-rescuer carries

5

When you are alone and you must move a casualty, use one of the following rescue carries:

▶ **pick-a-back**
  ▪ to carry a lightweight casualty who cannot walk but who can use his upper limbs

▶ **cradle carry**
  ▪ to carry a child or lightweight adult who is unable to walk

▶ **human crutch**
  ▪ to support a casualty who has one injured lower limb but can walk with help or someone who feels ill

Pick-a-back

Cradle carry

Human crutch

6

There are four casualties described below and three rescue carries you could use. Match each casualty with the carry you should use by placing the appropriate number into the boxes beside the casualty:

Casualty

☐ A. A four-year old has sprained a wrist and ankle.

☐ B. A heavy-set man has a slightly sprained ankle.

☐ C. A young girl has sprained both ankles.

☐ D. A six-year old has dislocated an elbow.

Carries

1. Pick-a-back
2. Cradle carry
3. Human crutch

A.2 B.3 C.1 D.2

Two-rescuer carries

7

When you must move a casualty and you have a helper, use one of the following rescue carries:

▶ **chair carry**

- to transport either a **conscious** casualty who cannot walk, or an **unconscious** casualty through hallways or up and down stairways (a third rescuer should assist when transporting on stairs)

▶ **two-hand seat**

- to carry a conscious casualty who can neither walk nor support his upper body

▶ **four-hand seat**

- to carry a conscious casualty who has the use of both arms but cannot walk

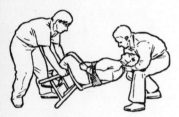

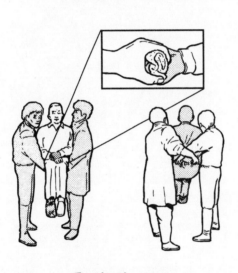

Two-hand seat

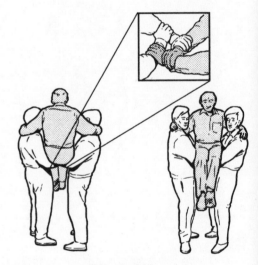

Four-hand seat

Chair carry

8

Mark each of the following statements as either true **(T)** or false **(F)**.

☐ A. An unconscious man can be transported down a spiral staircase most easily with a chair when three rescuers are available.

☐ B. It is best for two rescuers to use the four-hand seat to transport a girl who has a dislocated shoulder and a sprained ankle.

☐ C. A boy who has a large nail embedded in his foot can be carried most comfortably by two people using the four-hand seat.

☐ E. A casualty who has severe burns to his hands and feet can be carried by two rescuers using the two-hand seat.

A.T B.F C.T D.T

Blanket lift

9

The **blanket lift** is used by a team of rescuers (at least four) to carry a helpless or unconscious casualty. Before attempting this lift, be sure to **test the blanket**. Ensure that it will carry the casualty's weight safely.

Do not use this lift if you suspect the casualty has head/spinal injuries.

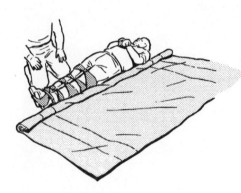
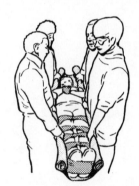
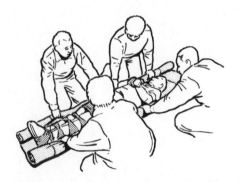

Blanket lift

10

In which situation would you use the blanket lift to move a casualty?

Check ☑ the correct answer.

- [ ] A. You must move a conscious casualty with an arm injury from the floor to a chair.
- [ ] B. An unconscious casualty with a suspected neck injury must be carried for a short distance.
- [ ] C. An unconscious casualty without suspected neck injuries must be carried for a short distance.
- [ ] D. You must move an unconscious casualty down two steep flights of stairs.

Drag carry

. . . .

11

In some situations, a casualty with suspected head/spinal injuries may be in immediate danger. If you are alone, move this casualty to safety using the **drag carry**. A drag carry involves **dragging** the casualty while **providing protection for the head and neck.**

You should do the following:

▶ stand at the casualty's head facing his feet

▶ crouch down

▶ ease your hands under the casualty's shoulders and grasp his clothing on each side

▶ steady and support the casualty's head and neck on your forearms

▶ move backward carefully and **drag** the casualty **lengthwise** only as far as necessary for safety

▶ if time permits, secure the casualty's hands together across his chest before dragging

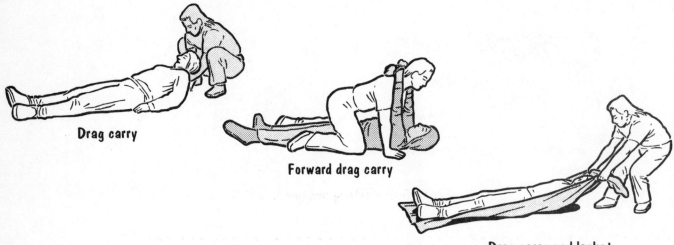

Drag carry

Forward drag carry

Drag carry on blanket

. . . .

12

Check ☑ the correct completions to the following statement.

To drag a casualty with suspected head/spinal injuries to safety, you should:

☐ A. Grasp his wrists and drag him head first.

☐ B. Stabilize his head and neck while you are dragging him.

☐ C. Pull him in a straight line.

☐ D. Move him as far as possible from danger.

Drag carry from a sitting position

. . . .

13

To remove **a sitting casualty** with suspected head/spinal injuries **from a life-threatening situation**, e.g. from a car, you should proceed as follows:

▶ free the feet and legs

▶ ease your forearm under the person's armpit on the exit side . Extend your hand to support the casualty's chin

▶ ease the casualty's head gently backward to rest on your shoulder while **keeping the neck as rigid as possible**

▶ ease your other forearm under the armpit on the opposite side and grasp the wrist of the casualty's arm nearest the exit

▶ establish a firm footing and swing around with the casualty

▶ drag the casualty from the vehicle to the closest safe distance, with the least possible twisting of the casualty's spine

Drag carry from a sitting position

. . . .

14

Following a collision, a fuel truck involved is near the edge of a ravine. A casualty is found in a sitting position in the driver's seat. You must move the casualty out of immediate danger.

Check ☑ the correct procedures listed below:

☐ A. Pull the casualty's legs out of the truck before supporting the casualty's head and neck.

☐ B. Support his head and neck with your hand and shoulder.

☐ C. Hold on tightly to the wrist of the casualty's hand closest to you.

☐ D. Quickly drag the casualty from the truck.

Objectives

• •

Following the video and upon completion of this activity book exercise, in an emergency situation, you will be able to:

▶ apply the principles of safety when moving a casualty

▶ move a casualty from a life-threatening situation

▶ move a casualty without a stretcher

For further information on rescue carries, please refer to:
First on the Scene, the St. John Ambulance first aid and CPR manual, chapter 15, available through your instructor or any major bookstore in your area.

EXERCISE 18

EYE INJURIES

Structure of the eye

1

The **eye** is the **very delicate** organ of sight. To give safe and appropriate care, you should know the **basic structure of the eye**.

Eyeball   – fluid-filled globe which is the main part of the eye

Cornea   – thin, transparent front of the eyeball that allows light to enter the eye

Eyelid   – movable layers of skin that provide a protective covering for the eye

Any injury to the eye is potentially serious and may result in **impaired vision** or **blindness.** Your quick response and the **correct first aid may help prevent permanent damage to the eye.**

Front view of the eye

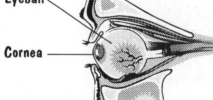

Cross section of the eye

2

Mark each of the following statements as either true **(T)** or false **(F)**.

☐ A. The eyeball is a hard, solid structure resistant to injury.

☐ B. Closing the eyelid protects the eye against entry of most foreign materials.

☐ C. The cornea is the delicate outer layer of the eye that can be seen from the front.

☐ D. An eye injury can cause complete or partial loss of sight.

☐ E. Loss of vision caused by an injury can often be avoided by prompt first aid.

A.F B.T C.T D.T E.T

Eye protection

3

Eye protection helps to prevent eye injuries.

At home, at play or at work, you should adopt the following **safety practices**:

▶ wear safety glasses or a face shield when you work with tools or dangerous chemicals

▶ keep chemicals off high shelves and take care to avoid splashes

▶ wear eye protection when you play sports such as squash, racquetball or hockey

▶ wear dark glasses with UV 400 protection or a wide-brimmed hat in sunlight or when light reflects from snow or water

▶ avoid looking into bright lights such as an arc welding flash or an eclipse of the sun

4

Which of the following illustrations show practices that would help prevent eye injuries? Check ☑ the correct answers.

☐ A.

☐ B.

☐ C.

☐ D.

☐ E.

Particles in the eye

· ·

5

Particles, such as sand, grit or loose eyelashes, may enter the eye causing pain, redness or watering of the eye.

Never attempt to remove a particle from the eye when:

▶   it is on the cornea

▶   it is adhering to or embedded in the eyeball

▶   the eye is inflamed and painful

To locate and remove a **loose** particle, you may need **to examine the eye**. Follow these **general rules:**

▶   warn the person not to rub her eyes

▶   wash your hands and put gloves on

▶   stand beside the casualty and steady her head

▶   spread the eyelids apart with your thumb and index finger

▶   shine a light across the eye, not directly into it

▶   look for a shadow of the particle

If the particle on the eyeball, **is loose and not on the cornea**:

▶   try to remove it with the **moist corner** of a clean facial tissue or cloth

▶   if pain persists after removal, cover the eye and obtain medical help

Note: If the casualty is wearing contact lenses, let her remove the lens—then continue with first aid.

Particle on the eyeball

· ·

6

A small grain of sand has entered a person's eye. The tears have not washed it away. Which of the following techniques should you use to remove this grain from the eyeball? Check ☑ the correct answers.

☐   A.   Give first aid for eye injuries with clean hands and in a good light.

☐   B.   Seat the casualty with her back to a lamp to keep the light out of her eyes.

☐   C.   Ensure that the object in the eye is floating freely.

☐   D.   Hold the eyelids apart and use a damp end of a clean handkerchief to lift out a visible, loose grain.

A   C   D

7

If tears do not wash away a small, loose object, and the particle is causing pain **under the upper lid**:

▶ ask the person to pull the upper lid down over the lower lid. The eyelashes on the lower lid may brush away the particle.

If your first examination does not locate the particle in the eye, you should examine under the eyelids.

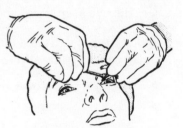

To examine under the upper eyelid, you should:

▶ seat the casualty facing a good light
▶ wash your hands and put gloves on, if available
▶ stand beside the casualty
▶ steady the head and ask the casualty to look down
▶ place a cotton-tipped applicator stick at the base of the upper eyelid and gently press the lid backwards, but **don't press** on the eye

Upper lid drawn up

▶ grasp the upper eyelashes between the thumb and index finger
▶ draw the lid away from the eye, up and over the applicator stick and roll the applicator back

If the particle is visible:

▶ remove it with the moist corner of a clean facial tissue or cloth

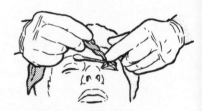

▶ if pain persists after removal, cover the eye and obtain medical help

Remove a loose particle from under the upper eyelid

(Left margin illustration)
Pulling upper lid down

8

From the following statements, select the correct techniques for removing a loose particle from under the upper eyelid. Place a checkmark ☑ into the boxes provided.

☐ A. Tell the person to pull the top eyelid over the bottom one if the grain is under the top lid.

☐ B. Stand near the casualty's shoulder on the injured side.

☐ C. Instruct the casualty to roll the eyeball upward.

☐ D. Expose the underside of the upper eyelid by rolling the lid back.

If you can see the loose object:

☐ E. Try to lift it out with the moistened edge of a clean tissue.

☐ F. If discomfort persists, place a warm wet pad over the eye.

A B D E

9

To **look** for a loose particle from **under the lower eyelid,** you should:

► wash your hands and put gloves on

► seat the casualty facing a light

► gently draw the lower eyelid downwards and away from the eyeball while the casualty rolls the eyes upward

If the particle is visible:

► wipe it away with the moist corner of a facial tissue or a clean cloth

► if pain persists after removal, obtain medical help

If a particle does not become visible during your examination and the irritation persists, do not continue your attempts.

► Cover the **injured eye** with an eye pad or gauze and tape loosely in place

► Obtain medical help **immediately**

Remove loose particle
from under lower lid

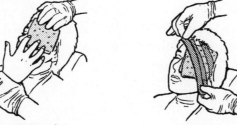

Covering the injured eye

Note: The reason for **covering the injured eye only** is to reduce psychological stress. If both eyes are injured, cover the eye that is most seriously injured. If both eyes must be covered due to serious injury in both eyes, e.g. intense light burn from arc welding, reassure the casualty often and explain what it is being done and why.

10

From the statements below, select the correct techniques for examining under the lower eyelid. Place a checkmark ☑ into the appropriate boxes.

☐ A. Tell the person to sit down.

☐ B. Seat the casualty with the back to a light.

☐ C. Pull the lower eyelid over the upper eyelid.

☐ D. Tell the person to roll the eyeball up.

If you are unsuccessful in finding the particle under the upper or lower eyelid, what should you do next?

☐ E. Repeat the examination until you find the object.

☐ F. Secure a soft dressing over the injured eye and take the person to the nearest medical facility.

Assist the casualty
to walk

A D F

Objects adhering to or embedded in the eye

Examining the eye

11

When a **particle** (small object) or a **large object** is stuck to or is embedded in the eye or in the soft tissues near the eye, **do not attempt to remove it.**

You should:

▶ warn the casualty not to rub the eye. It may cause additional pain and irritation

▶ lay the casualty down and support the casualty's head to reduce movement (if available, use a bystander)

▶ wash hands and put on gloves, if available

Depending on the size of the object, use one of the following bandaging techniques.

First aid for a small embedded object or adhered particle:

▶ close the casualty's eyelids and cover the affected eye with a soft eye or gauze pad

▶ extend the covering over the forehead and cheek to avoid pressure on the eye

▶ secure lightly in place with a bandage or adhesive strips

▶ keep the casualty's head immobilized

▶ obtain medical help or transport lying down

▶ give ongoing casualty care until hand over

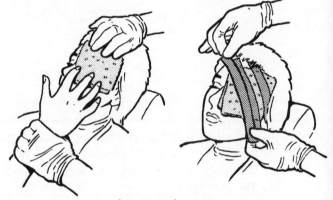

Covering the eye

Note: Do not try to remove a contact lens if there has been an injury to the eye other than a chemical burn.

12

Mark each of the following statements, dealing with first aid for an embedded particle in the eye, as either true **(T)** or false **(F)**.

☐ A. Ask the casualty not to touch the affected eye and to keep the head still.

☐ B. Use a cotton-tipped applicator to lift out a particle embedded in the eyeball.

☐ C. Place the casualty in a sitting position before you start bandaging.

☐ D. Secure a large, soft dressing loosely over the eye making sure that it does not press on the object.

☐ E. Cover both eyes to reduce the casualty's stress.

13

First aid for a large embedded object:

▶ lay the casualty down

▶ place dressings around the embedded object, using the "log-cabin technique" (building up dressings around the object) to prevent movement and tape in place

▶ ensure that there is no pressure on the embedded object

▶ immobilize the head to prevent movement

▶ transport the casualty on a stretcher to medical help

▶ give ongoing casualty care until hand over

How to prepare a ring pad

Log-cabin technique

Cup and bandage

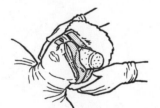

Taped cup

Ring pad bandage

Options for stabilizing an embedded object

How to prepare a ring pad bandage

14

From the following statements, check ☑ the actions which describe the correct first aid for a large embedded object in the eye.

☐ A. Build up dressings around a large embedded object to keep it stabilized.

☐ B. Make sure that the casualty's head is kept still.

☐ C. Place a gauze square with a hole in the centre over the embedded object.

☐ D. Cover the injured eye only, to avoid more stress for the casualty.

☐ E. Help the casualty walk to the nearest medical facility.

A   B   D

Wounds to the eye

15

A **wound or bruise about the eye** is always serious because there may be underlying damage.

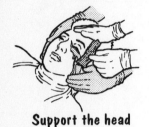

Support the head

A bruise to the soft tissues around the eye is usually the result of a blow from a blunt object. The bruise may not appear immediately, but there may be damage to the surrounding bones and internal structures. **A wound to the eyeball** from a sharp object is serious because of the possible damage to eyesight. **A wound to the eyelids** may cause **injury to the eyeball**. These wounds usually bleed profusely because of the rich blood supply.

To give first aid for wounds to the eye, you should:

▶ lay the casualty down, supporting the head, to prevent unnecessary movement

▶ wash your hands and put gloves on, if available

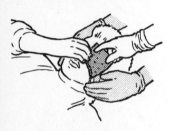

Cover the eye

▶ close the eyelid and cover the injured eye lightly with a soft eye or gauze pad and tape in place

▶ apply a dressing to the area if there is bleeding. This will usually control it

▶ **never** apply pressure to the eyeball

▶ obtain medical help or transport on a stretcher with the head supported

▶ give ongoing casualty care until hand over

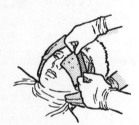

Tape gauze in place

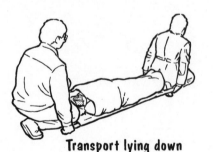

Transport lying down

16

From the following statements, select the correct first aid for wounds near the eye. Place a checkmark ☑ into the appropriate boxes.

☐ A. Place the casualty at rest and prevent the head from moving.

☐ B. Heavy bleeding from the eye should be controlled with direct pressure.

☐ C. When bleeding from an eyelid has stopped, leave the dressing in place and bandage the injured eye.

☐ D. You should bandage a bruised eye tightly to stop the internal bleeding.

☐ E. When giving first aid for wounds to the eye, you should avoid pressing on the eyeball.

Extruded eyeball

· ·

17

Severe injury may force the eyeball out of its socket.

Give first aid as follows:

▶ wash hands and put gloves on, if available

▶ **do not try to replace the eye into the socket**

▶ cover the extruded eyeball gently with a moist dressing and a cup and bandage

▶ obtain medical help. If not available,

  ■ place the casualty face up on a stretcher with the head immobilized for transportation to medical help

  ■ give ongoing casualty care until hand over

Serious injury could result if the casualty is not kept quiet and moved with great care.

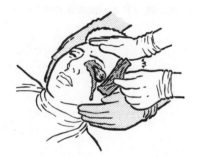 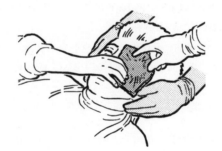 

Moist gauze applied   **Cup and bandage**

· ·

18

A hockey player's eye was forced out of its socket when a puck hit his eye. Before immobilizing the casualty on a stretcher, which first aid procedures should you take?

Check ☑ your choices.

☐ A. Support the eyeball with a firmly applied dressing and bandage.

☐ B. Lay the casualty on a stretcher face up.

☐ C. Apply a damp dressing loosely over the extruded eyeball and cover it with a cup and bandage.

☐ D. Secure a damp gauze square also over the uninjured eye.

☐ E. Obtain medical care immediately.

B   C   E

Burns to the eye

19

Eyes can be injured by **corrosive chemicals** (acids or alkalis). Chemical liquids or solids can cause **serious burns.** Casualties usually suffer intense pain.

The aim of first aid is to eliminate and dilute the chemical immediately. **You must act quickly!**

- ▶ Wash hands and put gloves on, if available
- ▶ Sit the casualty down with the head tilted back and turned slightly toward the injured side

If the chemical that entered the eye is a **dry powder**, you should first:

- ▶ brush the chemical away from the eye with a clean, dry cloth. Do **not** use your bare hands
- ▶ protect the uninjured eye
- ▶ gently force the casualty's eyelids apart
- ▶ flush the eye with tepid or cool water for **at least 15 minutes;** flush away from the uninjured eye
- ▶ cover the injured eye with dressings
- ▶ when both eyes are affected, cover only the more seriously injured eye, unless the casualty is more comfortable with both eyes covered
- ▶ get **immediate** medical help

Note: ▶ If the casualty wears contact lenses, ask her to remove them after flushing. If unable to do so, make sure medical help is notified.

▶ Proper eye irrigation equipment should be near at hand when there is a high risk of eye injury from chemicals.

Commercial eyewash bottle

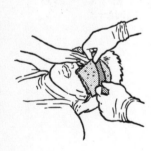

20

Corrosive lime powder has blown into a person's eyes. Place the following first aid steps into the correct order of performance by placing the appropriate number in the boxes provided.

- ☐ A. Guide the person to an eye wash fountain and flush her eyes for approximately a quarter of an hour.
- ☐ B. Quickly remove any loose, dry powder from the face.
- ☐ C. Get the casualty to a medical facility immediately.
- ☐ D. Tape gauze squares over the eye which is more seriously hurt.

A.2 B.1 C.4 D.3

Intense light burns

21

Burns to the eyes may be **caused by intense light** such as sunlight reflecting off snow, arc welder's flash or laser beams. Intense light burns **may not be painful at first** but may become very painful several hours after exposure.

When a casualty complains of burning in the eyes after exposure to bright, intense light, you should:

- ► wash hands and put gloves on, if available
- ► cover both eyes with thick, moist, cool dressings
- ► secure them in place (tape or narrow bandage)
- ► reassure the casualty as she is temporarily blinded
- ► obtain medical help
- ► give ongoing casualty care until hand over

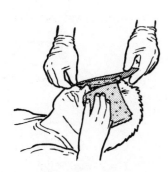
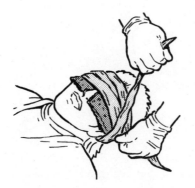
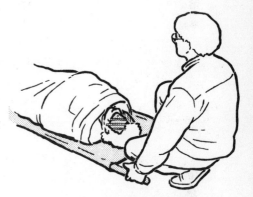

Cover eyes with moist gauze and tape in place   *or*   **Secure moist gauze pads in place with narrow bandages**   **Transport with both eyes covered**

22

A welder suffers light burns to her eyes when she is not wearing her face shield. What first aid should you give?

Check ☑ the correct answer.

☐ A. Apply dry sterile dressings and take the casualty to medical aid.

☐ B. Place the casualty at rest in a cool darkened room until her pain lessens.

☐ C. Keep her eyes uncovered and allow the tears to cool them.

☐ D. Secure cool compresses to the eyes and transport the casualty to a medical facility.

Heat burns to the eyelids

. . . .

23

When a casualty suffers burns to the face from fire, the eyes usually close as a natural reflex to protect the eyes. **Eyelids** may be burned and **need special care.**

First aid for burned eyelids:

▶ wash hands and put gloves on, if available

▶ cover the eyelids with moist, cool dressings

▶ secure in place

▶ call for medical help immediately

▶ give ongoing casualty care until hand over

Remember—when there is an injury to an eyelid, there may also be an injury to the eyeball.

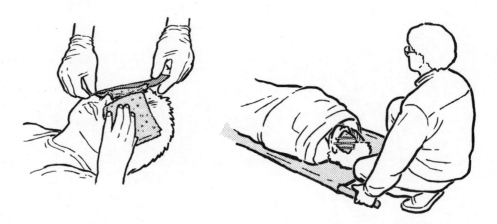

Cover both eyes with
moist gauze

Transport lying down

. . . .

24

Mark each of the following statements as either true **(T)** or false **(F).**

☐ A. Burns to the eyelids are not considered serious and don't require medical treatment.

☐ B. Part of the first aid for burned eyelids is to apply several layers of dressings which have been soaked in cool water.

☐ C. Nature protects the eyeballs from heat by cooling them with tears.

☐ D. The application of cool, damp dressings to burned eyelids reduces the skin temperature and relieves pain.

A.F B.T C.F D.T

Eye injuries—review

25

1. A person complains of a dust particle under her upper eyelid. Which of the illustrations below show the correct first aid procedures?
   Check ☑ your answers.

   ☐ A.

   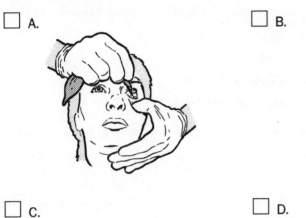

   ☐ B.

   ☐ C.

   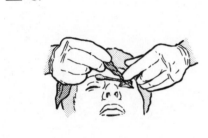

   ☐ D.

   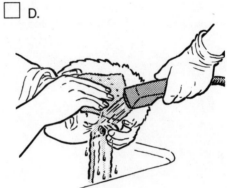

2. If you were unable to remove the particle, which of the following illustrations shows the correct eye covering you should use?
   Check ☑ your answers.

   ☐ A.

   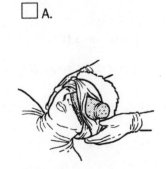

   ☐ B.

   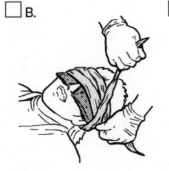

   ☐ C.

   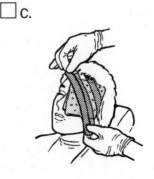

Objectives

· ·

Following the video and upon completion of this activity book exercise, in an emergency situation, you will be able to:

▶ take measures to prevent eye injuries

▶ provide first aid for foreign objects in the eye

▶ provide first aid for wounds in and around the eye

▶ provide first aid for burns to the eye

For further information on first aid for eye injuries, please refer to:
First on the Scene, the St. John Ambulance first aid and CPR manual, chapter 6, available through your instructor or any major bookstore in your area.

EXERCISE 19
BURNS

The skin

1

A basic knowledge of the skin and underlying tissues will help you to understand the serious damage **burns** can do and **to give appropriate first aid.**

Depending on the depth of the burn, the following tissues can be damaged:

▶ top layer of the skin (epidermis)
▶ second layer of the skin (dermis)
▶ fatty tissue
▶ muscle tissue

The skin **protects** the body against injury, extreme temperatures and infection.

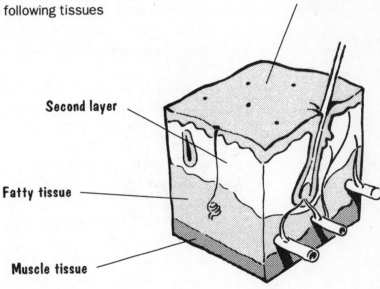

Top layer

Second layer

Fatty tissue

Muscle tissue

Skin and underlying tissues

2

Mark each statement below as true **(T)** or false **(F)**.

☐ A. Burns first destroy the outer part of the skin.
☐ B. The skin guards the body against outside damage.
☐ C. The skin is not affected by very hot temperatures.
☐ D. Burns break the skin and can cause serious problems.

A.T B.T C.F D.T

Prevention of burns

3

Burns are a leading cause of injury in the home, particularly among elderly people and young children. The diagrams below show you **dangerous situations** that may result in a burn.

Prevent burns by paying attention to the symbols shown on labels of hazardous products . . .

Danger corrosive   **Danger flammable**   **Danger explosive**   **Danger radiation**

and by adopting the following **safety measures:**

▶ use hand protection when you touch hot objects or work with corrosive chemicals

▶ keep electric equipment in good repair

▶ store flammable materials in a well-ventilated area

▶ clearly label corrosive and flammable chemicals or radioactive materials and store them in a safe place

▶ do not smoke in bed

▶ supervise children and elderly persons around hot stoves and when bathing

▶ install smoke alarms and fire extinguishers in your home and check them as suggested by the manufacturer

▶ develop and practise a fire escape plan

▶ wear protective clothing when exposed to radiation

▶ protect yourself from sunburn by wearing a hat and sunscreen lotion

▶ wear sunglasses when outside in bright light

▶ be cautious around open fires

▶ wear non-flammable clothing

Types of burns

4

Burns cause damage to the skin and other underlying tissues.

The types of burns are grouped by their mechanism of injury (cause):

▶ **heat** – dry heat
  – moist heat
  – friction
▶ **corrosive chemicals**
▶ **electric current**
▶ **radiation** – sun rays
  – radioactive materials

Dry heat

Friction

Moist heat

Corrosive chemicals

Electric current

5

In each of the following situations, a person is burned. Match each burn with one of the five causes by writing the appropriate number into the squares provided.

Sun rays

Situations	Causes
☐ A. A girl gets a sunburn while sleeping on the beach.	1. Dry heat
☐ B. A child in the bath is burned by hot water.	2. Moist heat
☐ C. A mechanic spills battery acid on his arm.	3. Corrosive chemicals
☐ D. A man receives burns when he uses a frayed electric cord.	4. Friction
☐ E. A woman is burned as a fire starts in the frying pan.	5. Electric current
☐ F. A boy's hands are burned when he loses his grip on a heavy rope.	6. Radiation

Radioactive materials

A.6 B.2 C.3 D.5 E.1 F.4

Signs and symptoms of burns

6

Signs and symptoms of burns depend on the depth of the burn. The **depth** of a burn is described as the degree of the burn.

First degree burn:

is a superficial burn; only the top layer of the skin is damaged.

You may see:

▶ reddened, dry skin, slight swelling

The casualty may complain of:

▶ pain ranging from mild to severe

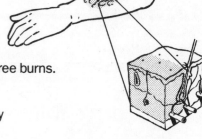

First degree burn

Second degree burn:

is a partial thickness burn; the second layer and the top layer are damaged

You may see:

▶ raw, moist skin, from white to cherry red, blisters with weeping clear fluid

The casualty may complain of:

▶ extreme pain

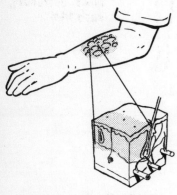

Second degree burn

Third degree burn:

is a deep burn with the full thickness of the skin destroyed; damage may also extend into the underlaying layers of nerves, muscles and fatty tissue. Third degree burns are often accompanied by very painful second degree burns.

You may see:

▶ white, waxy skin, becoming dry and leathery

▶ charred skin and underlaying tissues

The casualty may complain of:

▶ very little or no pain in the deeply burned area

Third degree burn

7

Mark each statement below as true (**T**) or false (**F**).

☐ A. A casualty with a burn covering the surface of the forearm may suffer severe pain.

☐ B. Burns are classified according to the amount of skin surface burned.

☐ C. In a first degree burn the skin will show many blisters.

☐ D. Where the burn is very deep and the nerves are damaged, the casualty may not feel any pain.

☐ E. Blackened skin layers indicate a deep burn.

A.T B.F C.F D.T E.T

Seriousness of a burn

8

The seriousness of a burn depends on the:

▶ degree or depth of the burn

▶ amount of body surface burned

This can be determined by the **rule of nines** by dividing the body into multiples of nine. The larger the surface burned, the more serious is the burn.

▶ location of the burn

▶ age of the casualty

Medical help is always required when the burn:

▶ is deep

▶ covers a large area

▶ is located on the face, mouth or throat and can interfere with breathing

▶ is caused by chemicals or an electric current

▶ involves an infant or elderly person

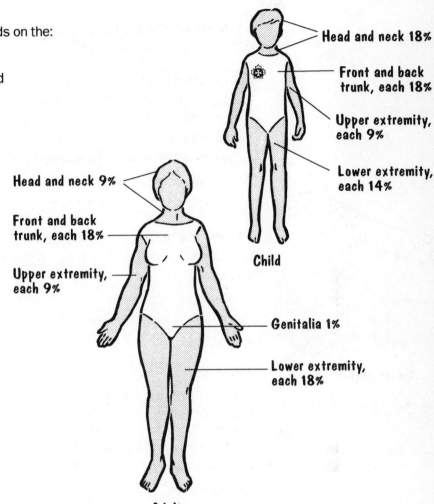

Head and neck 18%

Front and back trunk, each 18%

Upper extremity, each 9%

Lower extremity, each 14%

Child

Head and neck 9%

Front and back trunk, each 18%

Upper extremity, each 9%

Genitalia 1%

Lower extremity, each 18%

Adult

9

Which of the burn casualties described below would require immediate medical help?

Check ☑ the correct answers.

☐ A. A man splashes acid on his arms, neck and chest.

☐ B. A ten month old baby spilled boiling water over both his arms.

☐ C. A woman burns her hand on a hot kitchen stove.

☐ D. An 80-year old man burns his thigh and arm on a wood stove.

☐ E. After sunbathing a young girl has reddish skin on her back that is slightly swollen and painful.

☐ F. A teenager has difficulties swallowing after gulping down a cup of steaming hot tea.

A B D F

Smoke inhalation

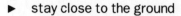

10

The air passages and the lungs can be seriously damaged by inhaling smoke from a fire.

To reduce the risk of smoke inhalation:

▶ stay close to the ground

▶ cover your mouth and nose with a wet cloth

▶ get out of the area as quickly as possible

▶ in industrial fires, don't enter the fire area without the proper safety equipment

Cover your mouth and nose with a wet cloth

Stay close to the ground

If your clothing catches fire:

▶ **STOP** moving—don't run

▶ **DROP** to the ground

▶ **ROLL** several times to put the flames out

STOP

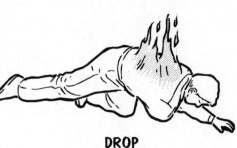

DROP

ROLL

11

You are trying to escape from of a room engulfed in flames. Your jacket has started to burn. Which of the following actions should you take to prevent serious burn damage to yourself?

From the options below, check ☑ the correct answers.

☐ A. Roll on the floor if your clothes are on fire.

☐ B. Get up and run towards the door.

☐ C. Crawl on the floor towards the door.

☐ D. Breath through a moist handkerchief.

☐ E. Open the windows for more fresh air.

A C D

First aid for heat burns

12

When you get burned, **immediately cool the burned area:**

▶ immerse the burned part in **cool water** until pain is relieved

▶ remove jewellery

▶ loosen tight clothing before swelling occurs

If immersing the burned area is not possible, you should:

▶ . gently pour cool water over the burned area or

▶ apply a clean cloth soaked in cool water

Immerse in cool water

Cooling a burn will:

▶ **reduce** the temperature of the burned area and prevent further tissue damage

▶ **reduce** swelling and blistering

▶ **relieve** pain

When the pain has lessened:

▶ cover the burned area loosely with a clean, preferably sterile material

▶ secure the dressing, ensuring that the tape does **not** touch the burned area.

▶ obtain medical help

Gently pour cool water over the burned area

or

13

Check ☑ the correct answer **to each of the following questions**.

You have just burned your hand on a hot stove. Which of the following actions should you do **first** to relieve your pain and avoid more injury to the burned area?

☐ A. Soak your hand in a sink filled with lukewarm water.

☐ B. Cover the burned part with an adhesive dressing.

☐ C. Soak your hand in a sink filled with cool water.

☐ D. Take off any rings from your fingers.

Cover with wet, cool cloth

A man received a burn to his chest and stomach area. How should you lessen his pain while awaiting medical help?

☐ E. Rinse the affected area with cool, salted water.

☐ F. Apply direct pressure to the burned area.

☐ G. Cover the burn with cool, moist cloths.

☐ H. Apply towels soaked in warm water to the burn.

Cover with clean material

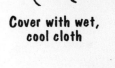

C   D   G

First aid for chemical burns

14

A **corrosive chemical** will continue to burn as long as it is in contact with the skin. To minimize the damage from corrosive chemicals on the skin, **speed is essential**:

▶ begin scene survey

▶ **immediately flush the area** with **cool** water

▶ if necessary, perform a primary survey and give first aid for life-threatening conditions

▶ flush during removal of clothing

▶ flush the area **for 15 to 20 minutes**

Remove clothing while flushing

If the corrosive chemical is a **dry powder**:

▶ remove contaminated clothing

▶ brush off any dry powder from the skin
  ■ **do not use your bare hands!**

▶ flush the affected area with cool water **for 15 to 20 minutes**

Following flushing:

▶ cover the burned area with a clean dressing

▶ obtain medical help

Cover burned area with clean material

Note: First aid for specific burns, e.g. from liquid sulphur, may vary from these general rules. You should know the chemicals used in your workplace and the recommended first aid.

Remove clothing while flushing

15

A workman has spilled a strong corrosive liquid on his arms and chest. What action should he take **first**?

From the following options, check ☑ the correct answer.

☐ A. Cover the affected area with clean, moist dressings and obtain medical help.

☐ B. Remove his shirt and pants, and then pour water over the body.

☐ C. Flush his upper body with cool water while taking off his shirt and pants and continue flooding for about 15 minutes.

☐ D. Take off his shirt and pants first, then pour buckets of warm water over his body for about 5 minutes.

First aid for electrical burns

16

Burns from an electric current may be more serious than they appear. As well as deep, **third degree** burns at the point of entry and exit, an electric shock can also cause:

- ▶ **stopped breathing**
- ▶ **cardiac arrest**
- ▶ **fractures and dislocations**

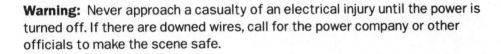

To give first aid:

- ▶ begin scene survey
- ▶ shut off the current, **or**
  get the casualty away from the electrical source, if safe to do so
- ▶ perform primary survey and give life-saving first aid
  - check for breathing and give AR if needed
  - check circulation and give CPR if there is no pulse
- ▶ cover the entry and exit wounds with clean dry dressings
- ▶ steady and support fractures and/or dislocations
- ▶ obtain medical help

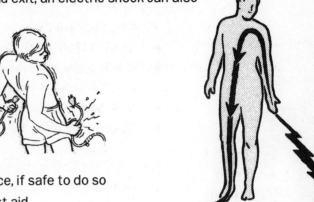

Electric current

Warning: Never approach a casualty of an electrical injury until the power is turned off. If there are downed wires, call for the power company or other officials to make the scene safe.

**Shut off the power
at the source**

17

Mark each of the following statements as true **(T)** or false **(F)**.

- ☐ A. There will usually be only one deep wound from an electrical burn.
- ☐ B. When treating a casualty for burns from electricity, the burned areas are the top priority for first aid.
- ☐ C. A casualty's breathing and heart may stop following an electrical charge through his body.
- ☐ D. In an electrical incident, you should first drag the casualty from the source of electricity.
- ☐ E. When a casualty has received a violent electrical shock, you should suspect injuries to bones and joints.

A.F B.F C.T D.F E.T

First aid for radiation burns

18

There is no specific first aid for radiation burns caused by radioactive materials. Workers involved with radioactive materials should learn the specific procedures and first aid for radioactive exposure. But first aid can be given for a radiation burn caused by the sun.

Radioactive material burn

Minor sunburn

► Sponge the burned area with cool water
   or cover the area with a cloth soaked in cool water

► Apply sunburn ointment or cream according to the direction on the label

   Caution: Some of these preparations may cause allergic reactions. Sunburn is the only burn to which an ointment is applied.

► Protect burned areas from the sun

► Do not break blisters

Major sunburn

► Give first aid as for heat burns

► If the casualty vomits or develops a fever get medical help immediately

Minor sunburn

Major sunburn

19

From the statements below, check ☑ the correct first aid for a radiation burn.

☐ A. Towels drenched in cool water are soothing when applied to sunburned skin.

☐ B. Blisters caused by a sunburn should be drained before applying wet towels.

☐ C. Persons with a sunburn should be asked to stay in the shade.

☐ D. People who have been exposed to radioactive materials should get medical help.

☐ E. Creams sold to treat a sunburn can be safely used by everyone.

A C D

Complications that may result from burns

20

A burn may be complicated by:

▶ **breathing problems**
- severe burns about the face indicate the casualty may have inhaled hot smoke or fumes

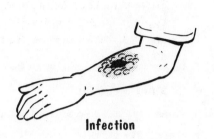

Infection

▶ **shock**
- caused by loss of body fluids and pain

▶ **infection**
- is a serious threat when the skin is burned and underlying tissue is exposed

▶ **swelling**
- particularly if jewellery or tight clothing cuts off circulation to the burned area

Precautions when giving first aid for burns

When giving first aid for a burn, avoid causing further injury and contamination.

▶ **DO NOT** overcool the casualty causing a dangerous lowering of body temperature

▶ **DO NOT** remove anything sticking to the burn. This may cause further damage and contamination

Take off rings before swelling occurs

▶ **DO NOT** break blisters

▶ **DO NOT** touch the burn with your fingers

▶ **DO NOT** breathe, talk or cough over the burn

▶ **DO NOT** apply lotions, oils, butter or fat to the injury

▶ **DO NOT** cover the burn with cotton wool, adhesive dressings or tape

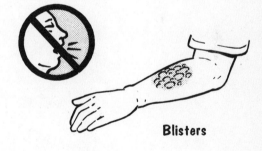

Blisters

21

Mark each statement below that describes how to prevent complications of burns as true **(T)** or false **(F)**.

☐ A. Watch for breathing difficulties of the burned casualty.

☐ B. Watch for signs of pale, cold, clammy skin and a weak, rapid pulse.

☐ C. Remove any rings before the tissue swells.

☐ D. Pull away a casualty's blouse that is clinging to the burned skin.

☐ E. Use your clean fingers to remove pieces of burned skin and clothing.

☐ F. Drain blisters before applying a dressing.

A.T B.T C.T D.F E.F F.F

Objectives

• •

Following the video and upon completion of this activity book exercise, in an emergency situation, you will be able to:

▶ take measures to prevent burns

▶ recognize burns

▶ provide first aid for burns

For further information on burns, please refer to:
First on the Scene, the St. John Ambulance first aid and CPR manual, chapter 9, available through your instructor or any major bookstore in your area.

POISONS, BITES AND STINGS

18 min

Causes of poisoning

Some substances are labelled as poisons with signs that you should recognize:

1

Poison

A **poison** is any substance that can cause injury, illness or death when it enters the body.

Many common substances can be poisonous and are not identified with any danger, warning or caution sign.

Examples of these are:

► tobacco

► alcohol

► some common household plants

► contaminated food

► medications when not taken as prescribed

Many substances not poisonous in small amounts are harmful in large amounts.

Poison Symbol

Danger Poison

2

Which of the following items could have a poisonous effect on the body?

Check ☑ the correct answers.

☐ A. Furniture polish

☐ B. A teaspoon of childrens' cough syrup

☐ C. A spoiled chicken stew

☐ D. Model airplane glue

☐ E. A large number of aspirins

☐ F. Street drugs

Warning Poison

Caution Poison

| A | C | D | E | F |

Prevention of poisoning

3

The best way to deal with poisoning is to prevent it from happening.

Many **poisonings in the home** could be prevented by paying attention to the symbols on the labels of hazardous products and the following safety measures:

► Read instructions on labels on containers before using medicines, chemicals or insecticides

► Keep poisonous substances in their original containers

► Ventilate area where toxic chemicals or gas combustion engines are used, so that fumes do not become concentrated

► Keep all medications, cleaning products, poisonous plants and other poisonous products out of reach of children

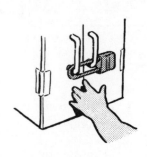

► Use child-resistant safety caps on medications and other products

► Teach children to avoid poisonous indoor and outdoor plants

► Prevent errors by carefully checking the **five rights** for giving medication:

- **right** medication
- **right** person
- **right** time
- **right** method
- **right** amount

► Safely dispose of outdated products

► Call your regional Poison Information Centre or your doctor for prevention and first aid information on poisoning before going to an isolated area, more than one hour away from a telephone

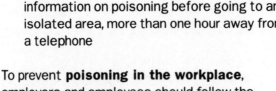

To prevent **poisoning in the workplace**, employers and employees should follow the government guidelines as outlined in the Workplace Hazardous Materials Information System (WHMIS).

4

Each of the pictures below illustrates a dangerous situation/mechanism of injury that could lead to poisoning.

Match each situation with the relating safety measure. Write the appropriate number into the squares provided.

☐ A.

☐ B.

☐ C.

☐ D.

Safety measures

1. Ensure fresh air in rooms where gas fumes are present.
2. Wear proper clothing when you may be in contact with poisonous substances.
3. Keep poisonous substances in original containers.
4. Store poisonous substances, including medication, safely out of the reach of children.

How poisons enter the body

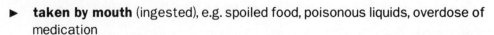
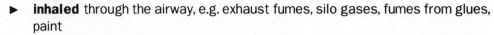
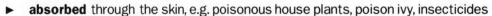

5

Taken by mouth

Poisons can enter the body in **four** different ways.

A poison may be –

▶ **taken by mouth** (ingested), e.g. spoiled food, poisonous liquids, overdose of medication

▶ **inhaled** through the airway, e.g. exhaust fumes, silo gases, fumes from glues, paint

▶ **absorbed** through the skin, e.g. poisonous house plants, poison ivy, insecticides

▶ **injected** through the skin, e.g. drugs, insect stings

Inhaled through the airway

Absorbed through the skin

Injected through the skin

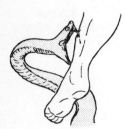

6

Match each of the following poisoning emergencies with one of the four ways the poison could have entered the body. Write the appropriate number into the squares provided.

Poisoning emergencies

☐ A. A swarm of wasps has stung a boy's face.

☐ B. A child is found unconscious beside an empty bottle of furniture polish.

☐ C. A man lies motionless beside the exhaust pipe of his running car.

☐ D. After a hike through the woods a woman, in her shorts, complains of severe itching on her legs.

Entry into the body

1. Taken by mouth
2. Inhaled
3. Absorbed
4. Injected

A.4 B.1 C.2 D.3

History of a poisoning emergency

. . . .

7

In any case of suspected poisoning, try to determine the **history of the incident**. There are **four basic facts** you need to know to give the appropriate first aid.

Ask the conscious casualty, ask bystanders or find out by checking the scene:

▶ **what** poison was taken?
  ▪ look for bottles, pills, etc; save vomit and give it to medical help for analysis
▶ **how** much was taken?
  ▪ estimate amount taken from the container and the contents left
▶ **how** did the poison enter the body?
▶ **when** was the poison taken?

Use your common sense to find out all you can about the poisoning incident.

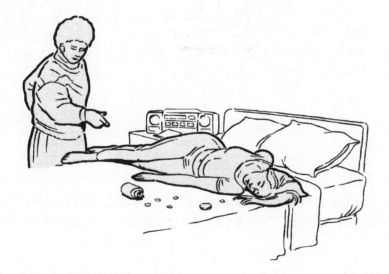

. . . .

8

You find a 4-year old playing in the garden with an open bottle of liquid pesticide in his hands. What information should you try to find out immediately?

Check ☑ the correct answers.

☐ A. Where did he find the poison?
☐ B. Did he drink the poison?
☐ C. Was the poison in a locked cupboard?
☐ D. What quantity of poison, if any, did he drink?
☐ E. If he drank the poison, how long ago was it?

B D E

General first aid for poisoning

9

When you suspect that a person has taken a poison, **act quickly** but do not panic:

- ▶ begin scene survey
- ▶ remove casualty from the source of danger. Be careful not to be harmed yourself
- ▶ gather any available information on the suspected poison
- ▶ assess the casualty's responsiveness

If the person is responsive:

- ▶ call the **Poison Information Centre** in your region or your doctor; give them any information you have and **follow their advice on first aid.** You will find the number of the Poison Information Centre at the beginning of your telephone directory

If the person is unresponsive:

- ▶ call medical help immediately
- ▶ perform a primary survey
- ▶ if you need to give **artificial respiration** and there is poisonous material or injury around the mouth of the casualty, use the **mouth-to-nose method** of AR with facial protection (e.g. mask or face shield)
- ▶ place the unconscious, breathing casualty into the recovery position and monitor breathing closely
- ▶ give ongoing casualty care until medical help takes over

Never induce vomiting in an unconscious or drowsy person!

Mouth-to-nose with shield

10

Mouth-to-mouth with shield

You find a casualty unconscious due to a probable overdose of sleeping pills. Which of the following actions should you do?

Check ☑ the correct answers.

- ☐ A. Get medical assistance as soon as possible.
- ☐ B. Check the casualty's airway and breathing.
- ☐ C. Provide mouth-to-mouth ventilations if the casualty stops breathing.
- ☐ D. Dilute the poison by moistening the lips with water.
- ☐ E. Leave the breathing casualty on her back and start looking for further clues of the incident.

A B C

Swallowed poisons

. . . .

11

The following may indicate that the poison was **taken by mouth** (ingested).

You may note:

▶ a half- or completely empty pill box, cleaning fluid bottle, or other substances

▶ discoloured lips

▶ burns in or around the mouth, e.g. from acids, alkalis

▶ odour on the breath, e.g. from petroleum-based products like kerosene, gasoline, furniture polish

▶ vomiting, diarrhea

The casualty may complain of:

▶ nausea

▶ abdominal cramps

The signs and symptoms may appear immediately or be delayed.

If the person is **conscious and you cannot immediately reach the Poison Information Centre or a doctor,** you should:

▶ begin scene survey

▶ perform a primary survey and give first aid for life-threatening conditions

▶ wipe the casualty's face to **remove** any poisonous/corrosive material

▶ **rinse or wipe out** the casualty's mouth

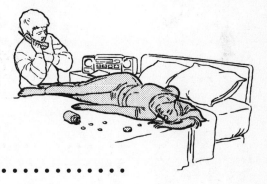

▶ **not dilute** the poison in the casualty's stomach. Some poisons, diluted, may cause more harm

▶ **never** induce vomiting except on advise of the Poison Information Centre or a doctor

▶ obtain **medical help** as quickly as possible

▶ give ongoing casualty care until hand over to medical help

. . . .

12

Mark each of the following statements as either true **(T)** or false **(F)**.

☐ A. Burns and traces of powder around the mouth of a toddler, could indicate a poisoning emergency.

☐ B. If you cannot get in touch with a medical authority, wash away all traces of the poison from the child's face to prevent more damage.

☐ C. If a person has eaten something poisonous and feels sick, immediately induce vomiting.

☐ D. In all cases of poisoning, the casualty should be taken to a medical facility as soon as possible.

A.T B.T C.F D.T

13

When you reach the **Poison Information Centre** or a doctor, they may tell you to give the conscious casualty **syrup of ipecac** to induce vomiting.

You may also be told, **not to make a person vomit** who has swallowed a:

▶ **corrosive** product, such as a drain cleaner; it will burn again when vomited

▶ **petroleum-based** product, such as kerosene; the vomit may enter the lungs and cause severe breathing problems

Syrup of ipecac can be bought in single-dose bottles (14 mL) at most drug stores without prescription.

Two or more bottles should be kept in a locked medicine cabinet and should be given **only** under direction of the Poison Information Centre or a doctor.

The **expiry date** on the bottles **should be checked** regularly and the bottles replaced if necessary.

If the content freezes or reaches a temperature above 30°C, do not use—discard and replace it.

If you don't have any syrup of ipecac, the Poison Information Centre or a doctor may instruct you to induce vomiting by giving the conscious casualty a **solution of 30–45 mL** (2–3 tablespoons) **of mild liquid detergent in 250 mL** (8 oz.) **of water** to drink.

14

Mark each of the following statements as either true **(T)** or false **(F)**.

☐ A. You should use ipecac syrup to make a conscious person vomit, only on the advice of the Poison Information Centre or a doctor.

☐ B. A doctor's prescription is necessary for buying syrup of ipecac.

☐ C. Vomit containing petroleum can harm the airway.

☐ D. A casualty who has swallowed a strong acid solution should be made to vomit immediately.

☐ E. You should give a soapy solution to make a person vomit only when told to do so by a medical authority.

A.T B.F C.T D.F E.T

Inhaled poisons

. . . .

15

The following may indicate that a poison was inhaled:

You may observe:

▶ strange odours, fumes or smoke at the scene

▶ breathing problems

▶ coughing

▶ unconsciousness

The casualty may complain of:

▶ headache

▶ dizziness

▶ chest pain

Inhaled poisons, such as gases should be cleared from the lungs as quickly as possible.

You should:

▶ begin scene survey. If the area is unsafe, do not enter. In a garage, open the garage door. Call for assistance, e.g. fire department

▶ **remove** the casualty from the source of gas or vapour to fresh air

▪ if the casualty is unresponsive, call medical help immediately

▶ do a primary survey and give first aid for life-threatening conditions

▶ monitor breathing closely

▶ obtain medical help as quickly as possible

▶ give **ongoing casualty care** until hand over to medical help

. . . .

16

You find an unresponsive casualty in a small room. The scene survey suggests that the person has inhaled gas fumes from a stove. You send for medical help. Which of the following should you do?

Check ☑ the correct answers.

☐ A. Remove the stove with the gas leak.

☐ B. Drag the casualty outside.

☐ C. Check for breathing.

☐ D. Begin artificial respiration if breathing stops.

☐ E. Call the gas company.

B   C   D   E

Absorbed poisons

17

The following may indicate that a poison has been **absorbed** through the skin:

You may see:

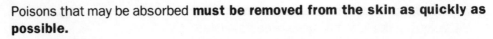

▶ poisonous plants, spilled insecticide at the scene

▶ reddened skin, blisters, swelling or severe burns

▶ breathing problems

▶ unconsciousness

The casualty may complain of:

▶ itching or burning of affected skin

▶ headache, dizziness

▶ nausea

Poisons that may be absorbed **must be removed from the skin as quickly as possible.**

You should:

▶ begin scene survey

▶ do a primary survey and give first aid for life-threatening conditions

▶ **flush** the affected area with **large amounts of cool water**

  ▪ if the poisonous substance is a powder, brush off excessive amounts with a dry cloth before flushing

▶ **wash** the skin with soap and water, if possible

  ▪ pay careful attention to hidden areas, e.g. under the fingernails, in the hair

▶ monitor breathing closely

▶ obtain medical help as soon as possible

▶ give ongoing casualty care until hand over to medical help

18

Check ☑ the correct completions to the following statement.

When a poison has been absorbed through the skin:

☐ A. The affected area may appear burned.

☐ B. The casualty should be given a large quantity of cold water to drink.

☐ C. The contaminated area should be flooded with a lot of running water.

☐ D. After the first flooding, the affected area should be cleaned with soap and plenty of water.

☐ E. If the affected skin was well cleaned, the casualty does not need medical help.

Injected poisons

19

When a poison has been injected through the skin:

You may see:

► disposable needles, injectable drugs, bee stings, etc. at the scene
► irritation at the site of injection
► breathing problems
► changes in pulse rates
► unconsciousness

The casualty may complain of:

► headache
► dizziness
► nausea

To reduce the spread of an injected poison throughout the body:

You should:

► begin scene survey
► do a primary survey and give first aid for life-threatening conditions
► keep the casualty **at rest**
► keep the limb with the injection site **below heart level**
► monitor breathing closely
► obtain medical help as quickly as possible
► give ongoing casualty care until hand over to medical help

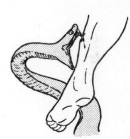

20

Mark each of the following statements as either true **(T)** or false **(F)**.

☐ A. When a poison has been injected into the lower arm, you should lay the person down and keep his arm lower than the heart.

☐ B. A person who has been poisoned by injection should be encouraged to move around to prevent unconsciousness.

☐ C. When a poison has been injected, your first concern should be to slow the circulation of the poison.

☐ D. A breathing emergency can develop following a bee sting.

A.T B.F C.T D.T

Animal/human bites

. . . .

21

Animal and human bites that break the skin may cause serious infection.

If you suspect that the bite was caused by an animal infected with **rabies, act quickly** and obtain **medical help urgently.** The infection can be prevented by immediate immunization.

Protect yourself:

▶ wear gloves when giving first aid and when you must handle the infected animal

▶ scrub your hands thoroughly after these procedures

To give first aid:

▶ **allow moderate bleeding** to cleanse the wound

▶ control bleeding if it is severe

▶ **wash** the wound with an antiseptic soap or detergent

▶ apply a dressing and bandage

▶ transport or obtain medical help as soon as possible

Each animal/human bite that breaks the skin should be checked by medical help.

. . . .

22

Which of the following statements are correct when dealing with an animal/human bite?

Check ☑ your answers.

☐ A. Let some bleeding get rid of the virus.

☐ B. Use cold water to kill the germs in the wound.

☐ C. Rabies is a potentially deadly disease.

☐ D. You can help to avoid a serious infectious disease following an animal bite by getting medical help without delay.

☐ E. It is helpful to identify the attacking animal to find out if it has been protected against rabies.

Snakebite

23

You may identify a poisonous snakebite by the following signs and symptoms:

You may see:

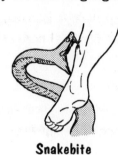

A poisonous snake will show two fang marks and a row of smaller teeth marks

- two tiny holes in the skin
- swelling and discolouration
- chills and sweating
- vomiting
- breathing difficulty

Snakebite

The person may complain of:

- burning in the area of the bite, followed by
- severe pain about the wound
- chills
- nausea
- general weakness

First aid is required urgently:

- begin scene survey—look for clues, call for help, etc.
- check for a clear airway and breathing, and give first aid for life-threatening conditions
- calm and reassure the casualty
- **place** the casualty **at rest** in a semisitting position
- steady and support the affected limb and keep it **below heart level**
- **flush** the bite area with soapy water, if available
- **immobilize** the limb as for a fracture and transport the person to **medical help immediately**
- monitor breathing closely

24

Check ☑ the correct answer to the following question.

To help slow the spread of poison through the body following a snakebite, you should keep an injured limb:

- ☐ A. Above heart level.
- ☐ B. Below heart level.
- ☐ C. Level with the heart.
- ☐ D. As high as possible.

. . . .

25

Warning!

Precautions in giving first aid for a snakebite:

◆ make sure there is no danger of a second snakebite to either you or the casualty

◆ **do not apply ice** to the wound, this could cause more damage

◆ **do not let the person walk** if there is any other transportation to medical help

◆ **do not give the person alcoholic** beverages

◆ **do not try to suck the poison** out of the wound with your mouth **or cut the bite mark with a knife**

◆ if the snake is killed, bring it to medical help for identification, but do not touch the snake directly

. . . .

26

Check ☑ the procedures you should follow when giving first aid for a snakebite.

- [ ] A. Place the casualty in a semisitting position.
- [ ] B. Make a cut at the puncture site and suck out the poison.
- [ ] C. Give the person a shot of brandy to calm him.
- [ ] D. Use soap and water to clean the wound.
- [ ] E. Keep the limb still and lower than the heart.
- [ ] F. Wrap an elastic bandage from the thigh down to toes.

Insect bites and stings

27

In most persons, an insect bite or sting causes only some painful swelling with redness and itching. **Bee and wasp stings,** however, may cause **severe allergic reactions** in some people.

Allergic reactions are recognized by the following –

You may see:

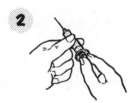
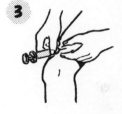

▶ hives and swelling

▶ vomiting

▶ breathing difficulty

The casualty may complain of:

▶ nausea

▶ breathing difficulty

When these signs occur, **obtain medical help urgently.**

While awaiting medical help, **give first aid as follows:**

▶ **assist** the person to take prescribed medication, if available

▶ if *EpiPen*® Auto-Injector or *AnaKit*® are available, follow the casualty's instructions and the manufacturer's suggestions

▶ apply **moderate constriction** above the bite site, if the bite or sting is on an arm or a leg

▶ keep the arm or leg **below heart level**

▶ **monitor** breathing

AnaKit®

EpiPen® Auto-
Injector

Bee sting

28

Check ☑ the correct statements below.

☐ A. People who are allergic to bee stings often carry their own medicine.

☐ B. Breathing may stop as a result of an allergic reaction to a bee or wasp sting.

☐ C. Frequent checking of the casualty's breathing is essential during an allergic reaction.

☐ D. An elastic bandage above the wound on a leg can slow the spread of the poison in the body of the casualty.

JAB

click

A B C D

29

To give **first aid** to the site of the bite or sting:

▶ **scrape** the stinger and poison sac carefully from the skin with a thin edge of a plastic card, e.g. credit card. Do not squeeze the stinger while removing it.

▶ **apply** rubbing alcohol, or a weak ammonia solution, or a paste of baking soda and water

▶ if the sting is in the mouth, give the casualty a **mouthwash** of one teaspoon of baking soda to a glass of water, or **ice** to suck

▶ if there is swelling in the mouth, and breathing difficulties, get immediate medical help. Monitor the casualty closely

▶ obtain medical help

Scraping stinger with credit card or knife

Bee sting

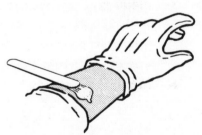

Applying paste of baking soda and water

30

Mark each of the following statements as either true **(T)** or false **(F)**.

☐ A. Discomfort and a stinging sensation are normal reactions to an insect bite.

☐ B. Baking soda mixed with water will soothe a sting.

☐ C. The stinger should be left in the skin to prevent further injury.

☐ D. The application of heat may help to reduce pain and swelling in the mouth.

Leeches and ticks

31

Leeches (bloodsuckers) are found in swamps, ponds and stagnant water. They attach themselves to the human body by making a tiny hole in the skin. Forceful removal of leeches may cause injury to the skin and infection.

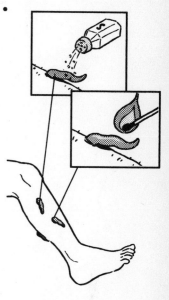

First aid for leech bites:

▶ **remove** the leech by applying salt, a lighted match, turpentine or oil to its body

▶ **do not pull** or **scrape** it off the skin

▶ **wash** the area around the bite

▶ **apply** a weak solution of baking soda or ammonia to relieve irritation

Ticks are found in forests and drop from leaves onto animals and humans. They bite through the skin and attach themselves. **Infection** from ticks may be harmful.

First aid for tick bites:

▶ wear gloves

▶ **grasp** the tick with tweezers as close to the casualty's skin as possible

▶ **pull** the tick away from the skin with an **even steady pull**

▶ avoid squashing a tick during removal; infected blood may spurt on you

▶ **clean** the area around the bite with soap and water

▶ wash your hands

▶ **keep** the tick for identification

▶ **obtain** medical help

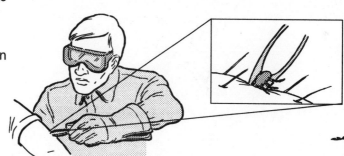

Wear protective gear when removing ticks

32

Mark each of the following statements as either **(T)** or false **(F)**.

☐ A. Leeches and ticks are able to fasten themselves firmly to the human or animal body.

☐ B. Using bare hands you should pull a tick from a person's body.

☐ C. A mild solution of baking soda and water will relieve the itch of a leech bite.

☐ D. A twig, heated in the camp fire, could be used to detach the leech from the skin.

A.T B.F C.T D.T

Objectives

• •

Upon completion of this activity book exercise, in an emergency situation, you will be able to:

▶ take measures to prevent poisoning

▶ recognize poisoning

▶ provide first aid for poisoning

▶ provide first aid for bites and stings

For further information on first aid for poisons, bites and stings, please refer to: *First on the Scene*, the St. John Ambulance first aid and CPR manual, chapter 8, available through your instructor or any major bookstore in your area.

EXERCISE 21

16 min

MEDICAL CONDITIONS
(DIABETES, CONVULSIONS, ASTHMA & ALLERGIES)

Diabetic emergencies

1

The body needs **energy** to function. The energy comes from sugar that the body gets from the food you eat.

Diabetes is a condition in which the body cannot convert sugar into energy because of **a lack of insulin**.

Insulin is a substance produced by the body to regulate the use of sugar. Normally there is a balance between the sugar used and the insulin produced.

A **diabetic emergency** occurs when there is a severe imbalance between the amount of insulin and sugar in the body.

Normal balance between insulin and sugar

2

Mark each of the following statements as either true **(T)** or false **(F)**.

☐ A. Sugar acts as a fuel for the body.

☐ B. Insulin is supplied to the body by way of the food we eat.

☐ C. Insulin controls the sugar level in the body.

☐ D. A person who has diabetes has a sugar imbalance because of a lack of insulin.

A.T B.F C.T D.T

3

Causes of diabetic emergencies

Diabetes is a condition in which the body does **not produce enough insulin,** causing the sugar level to be out of balance.

To balance the sugar level, a person with diabetes may take prescribed amounts of the medication, either by mouth or by injection.

Two conditions may result in a diabetic emergency:

Not enough insulin, causing a high level of sugar—diabetic coma (also called hyperglycemia)

Too much insulin, causing a low level of sugar—insulin shock (also called hypoglycemia)

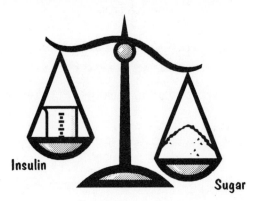

May be caused by:

▶ not taking enough insulin

▶ eating too much food

▶ doing less exercise than usual

May be caused by:

▶ taking too much insulin

▶ not eating enough food or vomiting

▶ doing more exercise than usual

4

Which of the following situations may lead to a diabetic emergency?

Check ☑ the correct answers.

☐ A. A diabetic person has regular insulin shots and watches his diet and exercise.

☐ B. An elderly non-diabetic person loves to eat sweets.

☐ C. A diabetic person misses dinner.

☐ D. A man forgets to take his prescribed amount of insulin.

☐ E. A young diabetic person competes in an unscheduled bicycle race.

How to recognize a diabetic emergency

5

A **conscious casualty with diabetes** might be able to tell you what is wrong. However, keep in mind that the person may be confused.

An **unconscious casualty** may be wearing a **medical alert** bracelet or necklace that will tell you that she has diabetes.

If the casualty cannot tell you what she needs, look for the following signs and symptoms:

	Insulin shock (needs sugar)	**Diabetic coma** (needs insulin)
Pulse:	strong and rapid	weak and rapid
Breathing:	shallow	deep and sighing
Skin:	pale and sweating	flushed, dry and warm
Breath odour:	odourless	like musty apple or nail polish
LOC:	faintness to unconsciousness developing quickly	gradual onset of unconsciousness
Other signs and symptoms	headache trembling hunger	unsteady walk nausea

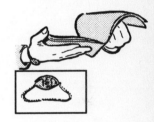

Medical alert devices

6

Which of the following actions will help you to assess the casualty's condition as a diabetic emergency?

Check ☑ the correct answers.

☐ A. Ask the conscious casualty about her condition.

☐ B. Look for some information on the unconscious casualty that identifies her as having diabetes.

☐ C. Keep asking the casualty questions, even if the response does not make sense.

☐ D. When the conscious casualty tells you that she has diabetes, ask whether she has had her normal food and insulin that day.

A   B   D

First aid for a diabetic emergency

7

The first aid for insulin shock and diabetic coma is the same:

- ▶ begin scene survey
  - ■ if the casualty is **unresponsive**, get medical help immediately
- ▶ do a primary survey and give first aid for life-threatening conditions
- ▶ place the unconscious person into the recovery position and monitor the ABCs until medical help takes over
- ▶ look for a medical alert device that will give you more information about the casualty's condition

If the **casualty** is **conscious** and knows what is wrong:

- ▶ assist her to take what is needed—**sugar or her prescribed medication**

If the casualty is **confused** about what is required:

- ▶ give her something sweet to eat or drink and get medical help

Unresponsive casualty

Give something sweet

Shock position

8

Which of the following actions should you take when a diabetic emergency occurs?

Check ☑ the correct answers.

- ☐ A. Give a conscious diabetic person several glasses of cool water to drink.
- ☐ B. Give a conscious casualty candy or orange juice if she is not sure what she needs.
- ☐ C. Send someone to telephone for medical help if the sweetened drink does not improve the casualty's condition.
- ☐ D. Place an unconscious diabetic person in the best position to ensure an open airway.
- ☐ E. Help a conscious casualty to take her medication if she says she needs it and asks for your assistance.

How to recognize an epileptic seizure

9

Epilepsy is a disorder of the nervous system. It may result in recurring convulsions, called **epileptic seizures,** involving partial or complete loss of consciousness. In most cases epilepsy is controlled by medication and seizures don't happen often. An **epileptic seizure** may come on **suddenly** and **be very brief.**

Any of the following signs and symptoms will help you to identify a major epileptic seizure—

You may see:

► the casualty falling to the floor
► sudden loss of consciousness
► noisy breathing
► frothing at the mouth
► grinding of teeth
► convulsions (uncontrollable muscle contractions) with arching of the back
► the casualty may loose control over bladder and bowel functions

Some casualties may complain of:

► a sensation such as a sound, smell or feeling of movement in the body that tells them that a seizure is about to occur. This is called an **aura**.

Aura

On regaining consciousness the person may be unaware of recent events and be confused and very tired.

10

Mark each of the following statements as either true **(T)** or false **(F)**.

☐ A. A person with epilepsy always experiences a feeling that convulsions are about to happen.
☐ B. Epileptic seizures are usually of short duration and may occur at any time.
☐ C. A person who has passed out during the seizure may not remember the incident on recovery.
☐ D. A person's mouth is usually dry and hangs open during an epileptic seizure.
☐ E. During a seizure, the person has no control over his movements and may gasp for air.

A.F B.T C.T D.F E.T

First aid for an epileptic seizure

11

The **aim of first aid** for an epileptic seizure is to protect the casualty from injury during the period of convulsions.

You should:

▶ begin scene survey

▶ clear the area of hard or sharp objects that could cause injury

▶ clear the area of onlookers to **ensure privacy** for the casualty

▶ **guide** but **do not restrict** movement

▶ carefully loosen tight clothing

▶ turn the casualty gently to the side with the face turned slightly downward. This will allow for drainage and prevent her tongue from falling back into her throat

▶ **do not** attempt to force the casualty's mouth open or to put anything between her teeth

When convulsions have stopped:

▶ place her into the recovery position and wipe away any fluids from the mouth and nose

▶ do a secondary survey to see if the casualty was injured during the seizure

▶ give ongoing casualty care, monitor breathing and allow her to rest

The casualty usually recovers quickly. If you know the convulsions were caused by epilepsy, you do not need to call medical help.

Call for medical help:

▶ if a second seizure occurs within minutes

▶ if the casualty is unconscious for more than five minutes

▶ if it is the person's first seizure or the cause is unknown

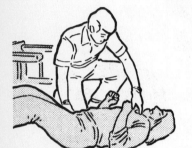

Make area safe

Place casualty onto side to allow for drainage

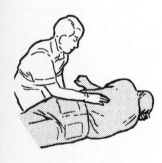

Recovery position

12

A woman in a crowded store suddenly falls to the floor and goes into convulsions. What should you do?

Check ☑ the correct answers.

☐ A. Tell the bystanders to form a circle around the woman.

☐ B. Clear away all objects on which she could hurt herself.

☐ C. Hold her arms firmly to prevent injury.

☐ D. Watch her closely to ensure she is breathing.

☐ E. Position her to maintain an open airway.

B   D   E

Convulsions in children

. . . .

13

An infant or young child with a **rapid rise in body temperature** to 40°C or 104°F is at risk of convulsions. A fever emergency is when the temperature taken in the armpit is 38°C (100.5°F) or higher for an infant and 40°C (104°F) or higher for a child.

First aid for fever may prevent the onset of convulsions

Advise the parent/caregiver to:

◆ call the doctor immediately and follow her advice

◆ give acetaminophen (e.g. Tempra® or Tylenol® according to directions on the label)if the doctor can't be reached

◆ **not give ASA** (e.g. Aspirin®), it may cause Reye's syndrome, a life-threatening condition, in children and adolescents

◆ encourage the child to drink fluids

◆ sponge the child with lukewarm water for about 20 minutes if the temperature doesn't go down. Don't immerse the child in a tub

◆ monitor the child's temperature and repeat these steps if necessary

Fever convulsions can be recognized by the same signs as an epileptic seizure *(see page 21–5).*

First aid for fever convulsions is to:

◆ protect the child from injury. Clear the area of hard or sharp objects that could cause injury

◆ loosen constrictive clothing

◆ not restrain the child

When convulsions cease:

◆ place the child into the best recovery position for his age, with the head lowered and turned to one side

◆ reassure the child's parents

◆ obtain medical help

Remove clothing

Sponge with tepid water

. . . .

14

Which of the following actions should you take when a two-year old child is having high fever and convulsions? Check ☑ the correct answers.

To bring down the fever:

☐ A. Follow the doctor's advice.

During convulsions:

☐ B. Hold her arms and legs tightly so she won't hurt herself.

☐ C. Unbutton her shirt at the neck.

☐ D. Ensure that she is breathing effectively.

When the convulsions have stopped:

☐ E. Position her flat on her back.

☐ F. Tell her parent to try not to worry.

Asthma

. . . .

15

Bronchial asthma, often simply called, **asthma,** involves repeated attacks of shortness of breath with wheezing and coughing.

Asthma causes narrowing of the airways in the lungs which is due to:

▶ tightening of the muscles in the airways

▶ swelling of the inner lining of the airway (bronchi and bronchioles)

▶ an increase in the amount and thickness of the mucus

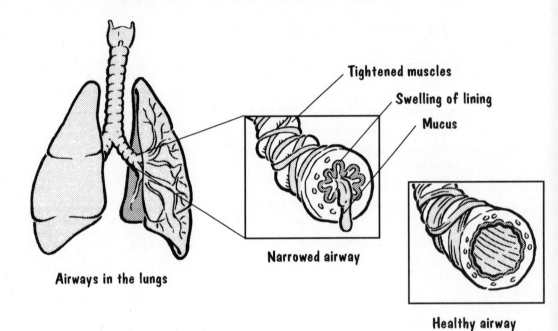

Tightened muscles

Swelling of lining

Mucus

Narrowed airway

Airways in the lungs

Healthy airway

. . . .

16

Check ☑ the statements below which correctly explain why the airways narrow.

☐ A. The lining of the airways becomes thicker.

☐ B. The mucus becomes thinner and more scanty.

☐ C. The muscles in the walls of the airways contract.

☐ D. More mucus develops and it becomes stickier.

Causes of an acute asthmatic attack

17

Asthmatic attacks are usually caused by exposure to certain **triggers.** These triggers vary widely among people with asthma.

Common triggers include, e.g.:

▶ house dust
▶ smoke
▶ pollen
▶ insects
▶ furry or feathered animals, e.g. dogs, cats, birds
▶ certain foods
▶ certain drugs
▶ a cold
▶ stress/emotional upsets

Although asthmatic attacks can be triggered unexpectedly, preventive measures can be taken by avoiding triggers known to cause an attack.

Triggers for allergic reaction/asthma

18

Check ☑ the correct statements below which indicate how you could help prevent certain triggers to cause an asthmatic attack.

☐ A. Regularly clean floors with a damp mop.
☐ B. Don't use rugs or drapes which collect dust.
☐ C. Avoid disturbing stinging insects.
☐ D. Allow your kitten to sleep on your bed.
☐ E. Use a down-filled quilt for warmth in the winter.
☐ F. Avoid grasses or flowers which have caused breathing problems for you in the past.

A B C F

How to recognize a severe asthmatic attack

19

Asthmatic attacks vary in how rapidly they begin, how severe they are and how long they last. A **mild** asthmatic attack can be annoying. A **severe** asthmatic attack can be fatal.

You can recognize a **severe asthmatic attack** by the following signs and symptoms:

► shortness of breath with obvious trouble breathing
► coughing or wheezing (a whistling noise when air moves through the narrowed airways) may get louder or stop
► fast and shallow breathing
► tightness in the chest
► casualty sitting upright trying to breathe
► bluish colour in the face
► fast pulse rate
► anxiety
► restlessness, then fatigue
► shock

20

Mark each of the following statements as either true **(T)** or false **(F)**.

☐ A. Shortness of breath eases as an asthmatic attack becomes more severe.
☐ B. All people with asthma wheeze during a severe asthmatic attack.
☐ C. Wheezing is the sound of air in smaller than normal airways.
☐ D. If a person with asthma is anxious, has sweaty, bluish/grey skin, is sitting and has difficulty with each breath, the attack is severe.

A.F B.F C.T D.T

First aid for a severe asthmatic attack

21

If the casualty shows increasing breathing difficulties:

You should:

► call for medical help immediately

► have the casualty stop any activity

► place the casualty in the most comfortable position for breathing. This is usually sitting upright, leaning slightly forward and resting on a support

► provide reassurance because fear will increase the breathing rate

► do not encourage drinking during an attack. Fluids may get into the lungs

► assist the casualty to take her prescribed medication if you are asked to do so (see next page)

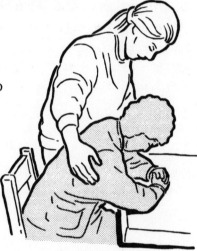

Position casualty

22

A middle aged man shows signs of a severe asthmatic attack with more and more trouble breathing. To help him, which choice of action should you take?

Check ☑ your choices.

Choice 1

☐ A. Call for an ambulance as soon as possible.

☐ B. Lay the casualty down to rest.

☐ C. Give plenty of fluids to loosen the mucus.

☐ D. Calm the casualty to relieve anxiety.

Choice 2

☐ A. Call for an ambulance when the casualty stops breathing.

☐ B. Have the man sit up to make breathing easier.

☐ C. Don't let the man have anything to drink.

☐ D. Encourage the man to breathe faster.

A.1 B.2 C.2 D.1

Assisting with inhalers

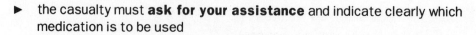

23

The casualty may be too weak or is breathing too rapidly to use the inhaler herself. You can assist the casualty to take her prescribed medication as follows:

Inhaler with collecting chamber and mask

1

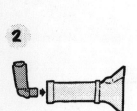

- ▶ the casualty must **ask for your assistance** and indicate clearly which medication is to be used
- ▶ ask for a nod as an answer to your questions to save the casualty from speaking
- ▶ ask if the container needs to be shaken and assist if needed
- ▶ remove the cap and hand the inhaler to the casualty for her to use
  - ■ it is not unusual for an asthmatic to take 5 to 10 puffs
- ▶ if assisting with inhalers is not possible, monitor breathing closely
- ▶ provide ongoing casualty care until medical help takes over

2

1

Shake inhaler

3

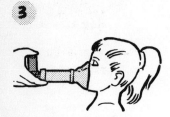

2

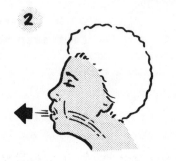

3

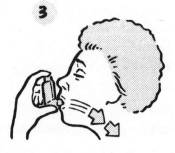

24

Mark each of the following statements as either true **(T)** or false **(F)**.

- ☐ A. You should give medication for asthmatic attacks immediately when you see that a person has problems breathing.
- ☐ B. Not all inhalers require shaking before use.
- ☐ C. If the casualty cannot speak, you should immediately give her the prescribed medication.
- ☐ D. Several puffs of medication may be required to relieve the breathing difficulties.

A.F B.T C.F D.T

Allergic reactions

. . . .

25

An **allergic reaction** is the response of a body with an abnormal sensitivity to substances that are normally harmless.

Substances causing allergic reactions **enter the body by**:

▶ swallowing (e.g. foods, medications)

▶ inhaling (e.g. dust, pollen)

▶ absorption through the skin (e.g. plants, chemicals)

▶ injection (bee/wasp stings, drugs)

The severity of an allergic reaction varies from minor discomfort to a **severe life-threatening type of shock** (anaphylactic shock).

Triggers

You can recognize a severe allergic reaction by any of the following:

You may see:

▶ sneezing, coughing and red watery eyes

▶ swelling of the face, mouth and throat

▶ laboured breathing with wheezing due to swollen tissues obstructing the airway

▶ a weak, rapid pulse

▶ vomiting and diarrhea

▶ pale skin, blueness or both

▶ changes in level of consciousness

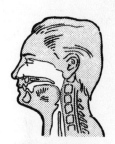

Inflamed airway passages

The casualty may complain of:

▶ tightness in the chest

▶ severe itching with hives (raised skin eruptions)

▶ dizziness

▶ abdominal cramps with nausea

An asthmatic attack is an allergic reaction that results in breathing problems.

. . . .

26

Which of the following observations may help you to recognize an allergic reaction? Check ☑ the correct answers.

☐ A. Smooth, pale skin on the body.

☐ B. Difficult breathing.

☐ C. Violent shivering.

☐ D. Puffy face and irritations of the skin.

☐ E. Indigestion and a loose bowel movement.

☐ F. Unsteadiness.

First aid for severe allergic reactions

EpiPen® Auto-Injector

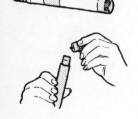

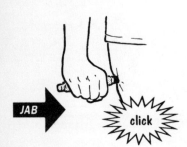

JAB → click

Ana-Kit®

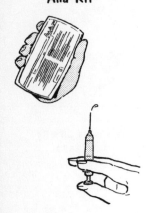

27

A person who has a known, severe allergy, usually carries this information on him:

Medical alert necklace

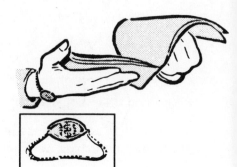

Medical alert bracelet

Give **first aid** as follows:

▶ send for medical help

▶ monitor airway, breathing, circulation (ABC's)

▶ maintain breathing and circulation

▶ check for medical alert information

▶ assist the conscious casualty to take prescribed medication, e.g. Ana-Kit® or EpiPen® Auto Injector. Follow the casualty's instructions and the manufacturer's directions. The medication will begin to wear off within 10 to 20 minutes

▶ provide care for shock until medical help takes over

Watch the casualty carefully. An allergic reaction can become life-threatening.

28

Check ☑ the procedures you would follow to give first aid to a person who is having a severe allergic reaction.

☐ A. Call for medical assistance immediately when you note signs of shock.

☐ B. If the casualty has an allergy kit, take him and the kit to a doctor.

☐ C. Ensure adequate breathing and provide artificial respiration if required.

☐ D. Monitor the person's condition continuously until medical personnel takes over or the person has fully recovered.

A C D

Medical conditions—review

29

1. You have a casualty who has asthma and is wheezing noisily. Which illustration below shows the best position for this condition? Check ☑ the correct answer.

☐ A.

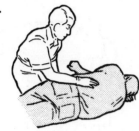

☐ B.

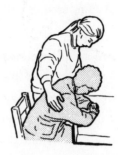

2. Which two illustrations below show the correct first aid for a diabetic casualty who has not eaten for a long time and is feeling sick? Check ☑ the correct answers.

☐ A. Help with an inhaler.

☐ B. Give something sweet.

☐ C. Turn into the recovery position.

☐ D. Call for medical help.

☐ E. Help with an allergy injection.

Objectives

• •

Upon completion of this activity book exercise, in an emergency situation, you will be able to:

▶ recognize a diabetic emergency

▶ provide first aid for a diabetic emergency

▶ recognize an epileptic seizure

▶ provide first aid for an epileptic seizure

▶ recognize convulsions in children

▶ provide first aid for convulsions in children

▶ recognize a severe asthma attack and provide first aid

▶ recognize a severe allergic reaction and provide first aid

For further information on medical conditions, please refer to:
First on the Scene, the St. John Ambulance first aid and CPR manual, chapter 12, available through your instructor or any major bookstore in your area.

ENVIRONMENTAL INJURIES & ILLNESSES

Temperature regulation

1

The human body normally maintains a temperature of about **37°C** (98.6°F). A healthy body can adjust to environmental changes and maintain its normal temperature by:

▶ **shivering** which helps produce and retain body heat when it is cold

▶ **sweating** which helps to cool the body when it is hot

However, when a person is exposed to extreme cold or extreme hot temperatures, the temperature control mechanism may break down causing **cold injuries** or **heat illnesses.** People in poor health, the elderly and young children are particularly vulnerable.

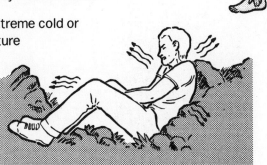

Temperature regulation

2

Mark each of the following statements as either true **(T)** or false **(F)**.

☐ A. Normal body temperature is 35°C (93°F).

☐ B. A healthy body is able to regulate its temperature when surrounding conditions are not too severe.

☐ C. Perspiring helps to keep the body from getting too hot.

☐ D. Trembling is nature's way of trying to keep the body warm.

☐ E. Very great cold or heat is unlikely to cause a person harm.

A.F B.T C.T D.T E.F

Cold injuries

3

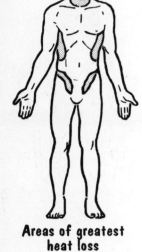

Areas of greatest heat loss

Anywhere in the world where there are cold temperatures people can die from cold exposure. Exposure to extreme cold may cause:

► **frostbite** – a local tissue damage
► **hypothermia** – a generalized cooling of the body

The **risk of frostbite or hypothermia is increased** when:

► low temperature is combined with strong winds. This is called windchill.
► the person is elderly, in poor health, or very young
► the person is in a weakened condition because of:
  ■ lack of food
  ■ fatigue
  ■ use of alcohol, tobacco or drugs
► clothing is wet (from sweating or immersion in water)
► clothing does not retain your body heat, e.g. cotton
► exposure to the cold is for a long period of time

4

You and a friend are cross-country skiing. From the statements below, check ☑ the situations that may increase your risk of frostbite or hypothermia.

☐ A. A strong wind bites into your face and you have no face protection.
☐ B. You are tired and have not eaten before going skiing.
☐ C. To warm up, you drink hot tea with your sandwiches.
☐ D. Your shirt gets wet from sweating and you feel very chilled.

A B D

. . . .

5

How to prevent cold injuries:

▶ **prepare for the worst conditions**
   – take extra clothing when outside in cold weather

▶ **stay warm**
   – wear several layers of loose fitting clothing that breathes, preferably wool. Silk, polypropylene and polyester pile are best next to the skin
   – wear windproof clothing or stay out of the wind
   – keep the head and neck covered

▶ **stay dry**
   – avoid getting wet, even by sweating

▶ **eat well**
   – eat high energy foods often at regular intervals

▶ **drink lots**
   – hot, sweet drinks are best, but cold water is fine if nothing else is available

▶ **stay safe**
   – limit the time spent in the cold
   – stay with a partner so you can check each other for signs of cold injury

▶ **avoid fatigue** – rest periodically in sheltered areas

▶ **avoid use of alcohol and/or tobacco**
   – these add to heat loss

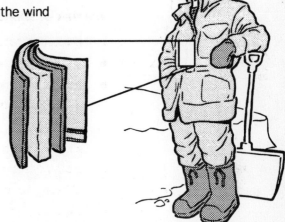

Properly dressed for the cold—wear multiple layers

. . . .

6

Listed below are dangerous situations that could result in cold injuries. Match each situation with a safety measure that could prevent the injury. Write the appropriate number into the boxes provided.

Situations

☐ A. Nothing to eat

☐ B. Weakened condition

☐ C. Poor clothing

☐ D. Wet clothing

☐ E. Long exposure

☐ F. No partner

Safety measures

1. Wear warm clothing and protect your head, hands and feet.

2. Carry an extra pair of woollen socks so you can keep your feet dry.

3. Use a "buddy system" to ensure safety.

4. Beware of becoming overtired and don't take alcoholic drinks.

5. Eat foods such as chocolate, nuts or raisins frequently.

6. Stay outside for only short periods when it is very cold.

A.5 B.4 C.1 D.2 E.6 F.3

Stages of frostbite

7

Frostbite is a localized cooling of the body. It may be:

◆ **superficial** – affects the entire thickness of the skin

◆ **deep** – affects the skin and underlying tissues

Superficial frostbite usually affects ears, face, fingers and toes.

You may see:

◆ white, waxy skin

◆ skin that is firm to the touch, but the tissues underneath are soft

The casualty may complain of:

◆ pain in early stages followed by numbness in the affected area

Superficial frostbite may progress to **deep frostbite.**

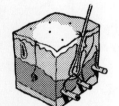

Superficial frostbite

Superficial frostbite

Deep frostbite is far more serious. It usually involves an entire hand or foot and affects the tissues beneath the outer layer of the skin. It may be recognized by the following:

You may see:

◆ white, waxy skin that turns greyish blue as frostbite progresses

◆ skin that feels cold and hard

The casualty may complain of:

◆ lack of feeling in the affected area

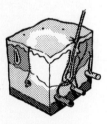

Deep frostbite

Lack of feeling

8

Frozen state

A frozen state of the casualty should be suspected when:

▶ the casualty is found in a cold location and is unresponsive

▶ the joints of the jaw and neck appear to be rigid when trying to open the airway

▶ the skin and deeper tissues are cold and cannot be depressed

▶ the entire body moves as a solid unit

Casualty is unresponsive

9

Indicate whether the person described below may have frost nip, superficial or deep frostbite or is in a frozen state. Place the appropriate number (1, 2, 3 or 4) into the boxes provided.

Frostnip (1), Superficial frostbite (2), Deep frostbite (3); Frozen state (4)

☐ A. A spot on the cheek is pale and does not feel as soft as the rest of the cheek.

☐ B. A foot is pale and greyish looking. The casualty says that he cannot feel the foot when he places it on the ground.

☐ C. A casualty is found in a snowbank. He does not respond when touched and the body feels hard and icy cold.

☐ D. One ear is white and the casualty complains of a dull feeling in the ear lobe.

☐ E. The tips of the fingers of one hand are colourless and cold. The surface of the skin feels firm but you can feel soft tissue underneath.

☐ F. The casualty says he does not feel it when you touch his hand. The skin feels cold, very firm and looks waxy.

☐ G. When you try to open the airway of an unresponsive casualty, the neck is stiff and the hard, cold flesh cannot be depressed.

☐ H. A spot on the nose is whitish and does not hurt.

A.2 B.3 C.4 D.2 E.2 F.3 G.4 H.1

10

First aid for frostnip and superficial frostbite

► Prevent further heat loss

► **Rewarm** the frost-bitten part **gradually** with the heat of your body by e.g.:

  ■ firm steady pressure of a warm hand

  ■ breathing on the frost-bitten part

  ■ placing the frost-bitten area in close contact with your own body

► **Do not** apply direct heat

► **Do not rub, or put snow** on a frost-bitten area

Human crutch

First aid for deep frostbite

A casualty with deep frostbite requires medical attention.

► **Treat the frozen part gently to prevent further tissue damage**

► Prevent further heat loss

► **Do not rub the limbs.** Do not allow the casualty to move unnecessarily

► **Do not thaw** the frozen part

► Obtain medical help

► Transport by stretcher if lower limbs are affected

Pick-a-back carry

If the casualty must walk –

► do not thaw the frozen limb (walking on a frozen foot is not likely to cause more serious damage)

► help the casualty to make walking easier

Two-hand seat

Rewarming with body heat

11

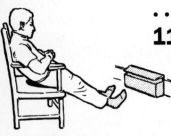

Indirect heat

Which of the following actions are the correct first aid for frostbite?

Check ☑ the correct answers.

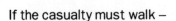

☐ A. Place your frost-bitten hands in your armpits to warm them.

☐ B. Warm a frozen foot quickly using a heating pad.

☐ C. If your ears become numb in the cold, cover them with your hands.

☐ D. Briskly massage frost-bitten toes with your hands.

☐ E. A casualty with a frozen leg should be carried, if possible, to the nearest medical facility.

☐ F. If a casualty with severe frostbite of the foot and cannot be carried to medical help, do not rewarm his foot. Help him walk.

A C E F

12

Thawing of a frozen body part should only be attempted when –

► medical help is not available
► the casualty is in a warm environment
► there is no danger of refreezing

If thawing of a frozen part is necessary:

► provide a warm, comfortable environment
► remove clothing gently from the affected part
► rewarm the frozen area in warm water at a temperature of about 40°C (104°F) until colour no longer improves. Warmer water will cause extreme pain
► carefully dry the affected part
► apply sterile dressings loosely on wounds and put sterile pads between toes and fingers
► give ongoing casualty care
► transport casualty lying down with legs slightly elevated

Rewarming

If a body is found in a frozen state:

► do not start CPR, if you are certain that a frozen state exists
► call for medical help, so that rewarming may take place under controlled conditions.

13

Check ☑ the correct answers to the following questions.

A. You and your friend are in a cottage in an isolated area without access to medical help. Your friend has a frozen foot. What first aid should you give him?

☐ A. Take off any wet clothes and expose the frozen part.
☐ B. Place his frozen foot under fast-running cold water.
☐ C. Soak his frozen foot in a tub of hot water of at least 44°C (111°F).
☐ D. When you have thawed his foot, cover any blisters with sterile gauze.
☐ E. Keep your friend warm and monitor his condition.

B. You come across a person lying in a snowbank. He is unresponsive to sound and touch. When you try to open his airway, the neck is stiff and the flesh is cold and cannot be compressed. You suspect that he is in a frozen state. What should you do?

☐ F. Get medical help but don't give any further first aid.
☐ G. Try to rewarm the casualty until he regains consciousness; then give CPR.

A D E F

Hypothermia

14

Stages of hypothermia

Hypothermia is a generalized cooling of the body, with body temperature falling below 35°C (95°F). It usually develops from exposure to abnormally low temperatures over a prolonged period of time. However, it can also develop in temperatures well above freezing. Watch for early signs of hypothermia and prevent it from becoming worse.

Hypothermia may progress from **mild** to **moderate** to **severe** if it is not recognized and first aid is not given immediately.

You may see the following changes in the signs as the casualty's condition becomes more severe.

Signs	Progressive stages of hypothermia		
	Mild	**Moderate**	**Severe**
Pulse	normal	slow and weak	weak, irregular or absent
Breathing	normal	slow and shallow	slow or absent
Appearance	shivering, slurred speech	shivering is violent or stopped, is clumsy and stumbles	shivering has stopped
Mental state	conscious, withdrawn	confused, sleepy, irrational	unconscious

15

Mark each of the following statement as either true (**T**) or false (**F**).

- [ ] A. A person who is wet and in the cold may develop hypothermia.
- [ ] B. A person in mild hypothermia will appear mixed-up and drowsy.
- [ ] C. Hypothermia becomes more serious as the casualty's temperature falls.
- [ ] D. A person in moderate hypothermia may have a rapid pulse but normal breathing.
- [ ] E. A person suffering from very long exposure to cold may appear to have no signs of life.
- [ ] F. A person in severe hypothermia will stop shaking.

First aid for hypothermia

16

The **aims of first aid for hypothermia** are to:

► prevent further loss of body heat

► obtain medical help as quickly as possible

When a casualty is suffering from hypothermia, you should:

Huddling

► **handle him gently** with the least possible movement

► remove him from the cold environment, e.g. water, snow, poorly heated housing to a warm shelter

► **remove** wet clothing and place the casualty under warm covers, such as a warm sleeping bag

► **protect him from the wind** by huddling with the casualty

► give the conscious casualty a **warm sweet drink**. Do not give alcohol or coffee or other caffeine-containing drinks

► **monitor** breathing and pulse

► if breathing is ineffective, provide assisted breathing

Sweet warm drink

17

A man is pulled from an icy lake and placed in a shelter. He is conscious and shivering. Place the following first aid actions in the **appropriate sequence of performance.** Write the numbers into the boxes provided.

☐ A. Wrap him in warm blankets.

☐ B. Watch his breathing and check his pulse often.

☐ C. Give him a hot drink with sugar.

☐ D. Take off his wet clothes carefully.

A.2 B.4 C.3 D.1

18

When the casualty becomes unconscious:

▶ obtain medical help immediately

▶ give artificial respiration if breathing stops, but handle the casualty gently. The slightest rough handling may cause his heart to fail

▶ ventilate at an appropriate rate for the age of the casualty

▶ **check the carotid pulse for 1 to 2 minutes** to ensure that even a weak, slow pulse can be detected

If a carotid pulse is not present:

▶ **give CPR only if it can be maintained** without interruption until medical help takes over

▶ if no medical help is available, continue to ventilate until the casualty is rewarmed

Never assume that a casualty in severe hypothermia is dead until his body is warm again and there are still no signs of life.

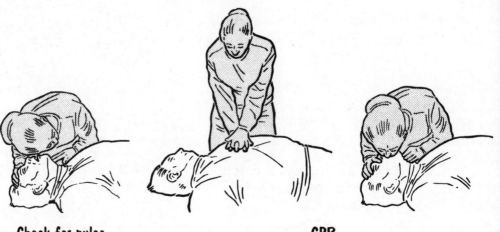

Check for pulse   **CPR**

19

You find a casualty unresponsive in an isolated, cold environment. To make sure to feel even a very slow, faint heartbeat, how long should you check his pulse?

☐ A. For 5 to 10 seconds.

☐ B. For 1 to 2 minutes.

☐ C. For about 3 minutes.

☐ D. For about 5 seconds.

First aid for cold injuries—review

20

1. Your friend has severe frostbite on both feet. You are in a remote area in a warm lodge, but without access to medical help. Which of the following first aid actions should you do? Check ☑ your answer.

☐ A. Help the casualty walk until his feet are rewarmed.

☐ B. Gently rewarm the frozen feet in warm water of about 40°C (104°F).

☐ C. Ask the casualty to rub his feet vigorously.

☐ D. Give the casualty a glass of hot rum to drink.

2. Which of the following actions would be correct first aid for a non-breathing casualty suffering from severe hypothermia? Check ☑ your answers.

☐ A. Take 1 to 2 minutes to check for a pulse (there is a very faint pulse).

☐ B. Handle the casualty gently and give CPR.

☐ C. Get medical help immediately.

☐ D. Handle the casualty gently and give AR.

1.B 2.A 2.C 2.D

Heat illnesses

· ·

21

Heat cramps, heat exhaustion and heatstroke are illnesses that are caused by:

► the body's inability to maintain a normal temperature of 37°C (98.6°F)
► long exposure to hot conditions
► overexposure to the sun
► lack of fluids to replace lost body fluids
► vigorous exercise or hard labour in a hot environment

To **prevent heat illnesses,** you should:

► expose the body gradually to a hot environment
► protect the head from direct sunshine
► drink sufficient water to replace body fluids lost through sweating
► avoid long periods of work or exercise in a hot environment

Drinking fluids

· ·

22

Which of the following precautions would help you to avoid illness from exposure to heat?

Check ☑ the correct answers.

☐ A. Take drinks when you are working in the heat.

☐ B. Avoid wearing a hat on a hot sunny day to allow body heat to be lost through the head.

☐ C. If you are not used to a hot climate or workplace, stay in the heat for only a short time.

☐ D. Take frequent breaks in a cool place when you are working or playing on a hot day.

A C D

Heat cramps

23

Heat cramps are painful muscle spasms caused by an excessive loss of salt and water during sweating. This condition is not serious and usually responds well to first aid.

You may see:

◆ excessive sweating

The casualty may complain of:

◆ painful muscle cramps in the legs and abdomen

Stomach cramps

First aid for heat cramps

When a person is complaining of heat cramps, you should:

◆ place her in a **cool place** to rest

◆ give her **water** to drink, as much as she will take

◆ obtain medical help if muscle pain continues

Giving
water to drink

Place in shade

24

A teenager playing soccer on a hot day complains of pain in her legs and abdomen. Which of the following should you do in giving first aid?

Check ☑ your answers in the boxes provided.

- [ ] A. Lay her down on the sunny playing field until the pain disappears.
- [ ] B. Give her plain water to drink, as much as she wants.
- [ ] C. Tell her not to worry and to continue with the game.
- [ ] D. Take her to a medical facility if she continues to complain of pain.

B   D

Heat exhaustion

. . . .

25

Heat exhaustion is more serious than heat cramps.

It occurs when excessive sweating causes a loss of body fluids and when a hot environment and high humidity do not allow the body to cool by sweating.

You may see signs of shock:

▶ excessive sweating

▶ cold, clammy, pale skin

▶ weak and rapid pulse

▶ rapid, shallow breathing

▶ vomiting

▶ unconsciousness

The casualty may complain of:

▶ blurred vision

▶ dizziness

▶ headache

▶ nausea

▶ painful cramps in the legs and abdomen

Excessive sweating

Painful cramps

. . . .

26

When a casualty is suffering from heat exhaustion, which of the following signs and symptoms may be present?

Check ☑ your answers in the boxes provided.

☐ A. The skin is whitish, cool and damp.

☐ B. The pulse and breathing are very slow.

☐ C. She tells you that she has a sore head and feels sick to her stomach.

☐ D. She has difficulty walking because her legs hurt.

☐ E. She collapses and does not respond.

27

First aid for heat exhaustion

The first aid for heat exhaustion is a combination of the first aid for heat cramps and shock.

If the casualty is fully conscious, you should:

◆ place the casualty at rest in a cool place, with feet and legs elevated
◆ remove excessive clothing
◆ loosen tight clothing at neck and waist
◆ give water to drink, as much as the casualty will take
◆ if the casualty is vomiting, give nothing by mouth, ensure an open airway and get medical help immediately

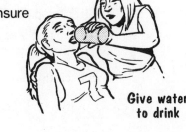

Give water to drink

Shock position

If the casualty is unconscious:

◆ obtain medical help immediately
◆ place the casualty into the recovery position
◆ monitor ABC's and give life-saving first aid as needed
◆ give ongoing casualty care until medical help takes over

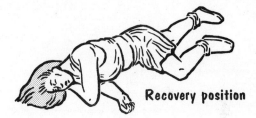

Recovery position

28

A woman working in a hot assembly plant complains of muscle spasms and is beginning to show signs of shock. If she is fully conscious, what first aid should you give her?

Check ☑ your answers in the boxes provided.

☐ A. Help her lie down in a well-ventilated area and place a folded blanket under her legs.
☐ B. Give her as much water as she will drink.
☐ C. Ensure that her clothing is snug and warm.

If the woman loses consciousness, you should:

☐ D. Place her on her back.
☐ E. Ensure effective breathing and circulation.

A B E

Heatstroke

29

Heatstroke is life-threatening. There are two kinds of heatstroke:

► **classic** heatstroke occurs when the body's temperature control fails
► **exertional** heatstroke occurs as a result of heavy physical exertion in high temperature

You may see:

► body temperature rising rapidly to 40°C (104°F) and above
► rapid and full pulse, becoming weaker in later stages
► flushed, hot, **dry skin in classic** heatstroke
► flushed, hot, **sweaty skin in exertional** heatstroke
► noisy breathing
► vomiting
► restlessness
► convulsions
► unconsciousness

The casualty may complain of:

► headache
► dizziness
► nausea

Dizziness

Flushed, hot, dry skin

Flushed, hot, sweaty skin

Elderly persons and those in poor health are more likely to suffer from heatstroke.

30

With the options below, complete the following statements by placing a checkmark ☑ in the boxes provided:

When a person suffers heatstroke, she may –

☐ A. Be in immediate danger.
☐ B. Appear red in the face and breathe with difficulty.
☐ C. Have a temperature of 35°C (95°F) and a slow pulse.
☐ D. Complain that her head hurts and she is about to throw up.

In **classic** heatstroke, she may –

☐ E. Feel hot to the touch and be covered with sweat.
☐ F. Feel hot to the touch but have no signs of sweating.

In **exertional** heatstroke, she may –

☐ G. Have cold and dry skin.
☐ H. Have hot skin, wet from sweat.

A B D F H

31

First aid for heatstroke (classic or exertional)

Heatstroke is a high priority emergency. **It is life-threatening.**

▶ Send for medical help immediately

To prevent permanent brain damage or death, you must **reduce the body temperature quickly.**

Immerse in cool bath

You should:

▶ move the person to a cool, shaded place

▶ ensure a clear airway and adequate breathing

▶ remove clothing

▶ **immerse** the casualty **in a cool bath** and watch her closely, or

▶ **sponge** the casualty **with cool water,** particularly in the armpit, neck and groin areas, or

Sponge with cool water

▶ **cover her with wet sheets** and fan cool air over her

▶ when the body feels cooler to the touch, cover her with a dry sheet

▶ monitor the casualty's temperature and if it rises, repeat the cooling procedure

▶ give ongoing casualty care until hand over to medical help

▶ place the unconscious casualty into the **recovery position**

▶ place the conscious casualty into the **shock position**

Shock position and air fan

32

A casualty is suffering from heatstroke. You have sent for medical help. While awaiting medical help, which of the following actions could you take to reduce her body temperature?

Check ☑ your answers in the boxes provided.

☐ A. Place cold, wet cloths on her forehead, the back of her neck, under the armpits and around her lower abdomen.

☐ B. Apply a cold dry towel to her forehead.

☐ C. Place cool, wet bath sheets over her body and circulate air around her.

☐ D. Soak her in a large tub filled with ice water.

☐ E. Place her feet in a pail of tepid water.

Recovery position

When the temperature has been reduced:

☐ F. Position her to ensure an open airway and watch her carefully.

☐ G. Leave her to herself to get a good rest.

Objectives

• •

Upon completion of this activity book exercise, in an emergency situation, you will be able to:

▶ take measures to prevent cold injuries.

▶ recognize cold injuries.

▶ provide first aid for cold injuries.

▶ take measures to prevent heat illnesses.

▶ recognize heat illnesses.

▶ provide first aid for heat illnesses.

For further information on first aid for cold injuries and heat illnesses, please refer to: *First on the Scene*, the St. John Ambulance first aid and CPR manual, chapter 10, available through your instructor or any major bookstore in your area.

EMERGENCY CHILDBIRTH AND MISCARRIAGE

Introduction to emergency childbirth

1

A basic knowledge of the female reproductive system and its relationship to the unborn child will help to give assistance during an emergency delivery.

▶ **Fetus** — the developing baby

▶ **Uterus** — the hollow muscular structure, also called womb, inside which the fetus develops

▶ **Cervix** — the neck of the uterus through which the fetus will pass into the vagina

▶ **Amniotic sac** — a fluid-filled sac, contained within the uterus, in which the fetus develops

Vagina   **Uterus**

▶ **Amniotic fluid** — liquid that surrounds and protects the fetus in the amniotic sac

▶ **Placenta** — large flat, spongy organ that is attached to the wall of the uterus and supplies the fetus with nutrients and oxygen from the mother

Fetus

▶ **Umbilical cord** — a rope-like structure that contains blood vessels and connects the placenta with the fetus

▶ **Vagina** — the muscular birth canal for the delivery of the infant

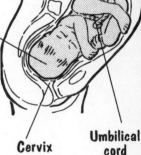

Cervix   **Umbilical cord**

2

Mark each of the following statements as true **(T)** or false **(F)**.

- [ ] A. The fetus is the unborn infant which lies in a fluid-filled bag inside the uterus.
- [ ] B. The infant takes in oxygen and nourishment from the amniotic fluid.
- [ ] C. During delivery the fetus enters the birth canal through the opened cervix.
- [ ] D. The placenta is attached to the fetus by the umbilical cord.

A.T B.F C.T D.T

Labour

3

Labour is the process through which the body prepares itself to deliver the baby.

The **early signs of beginning labour** are signalled by:

▶ regular rhythmic contractions at first mild to moderate strength

▶ breaking of the amniotic sac and the release of fluid through the vagina, known as "the water breaking"

▶ appearance of the "bloody show", consisting of blood and mucus, from the vagina

Normally the beginning of labour gives enough warning for the mother to be transported to a medical facility for delivery.

There are **three stages** of labour:

1. **opening of the cervix** (widening) brought about by increasingly stronger contractions
2. **birth of the baby**
3. **delivery of the placenta**

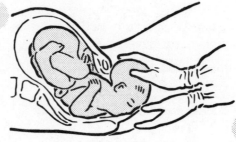
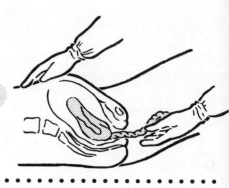

4

Which of the following are normal signs indicating that a pregnant woman is beginning labour?

Check ☑ the correct answers.

☐ A. A gush or trickle of watery fluid from the vagina.

☐ B. Frequent urination.

☐ C. A steady flow of blood from the vagina.

☐ D. Sharp pains felt in the abdomen.

☐ E. A pinkish discharge from the vagina.

Signs of imminent delivery

. . . .

5

Signs and symptoms of imminent delivery are:

▶ long, strong contractions, less than 2 minutes apart

▶ the mother's previous experience. If she says, the baby is coming, believe her!

▶ bulging of the vaginal opening and seeing the baby's head (crowning)

▶ the mother is straining and pushing down, feels as though she has to have a bowel movement

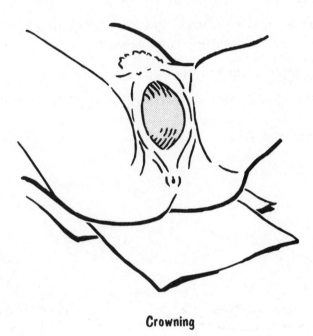

Crowning

. . . .

6

Mark each statement below as true **(T)** or false **(F)**.

☐ A. The urge of the mother to move her bowels is an indication that the baby is about to be born.

☐ B. Intense pain in short intervals usually means that the baby will be delivered very soon.

☐ C. When the baby's head can be seen through the vagina, there is still time to transport the mother to the hospital.

☐ D. A woman who has given birth before can usually tell when the delivery is about to occur.

A.T B.T C.F D.T

Preparation for emergency delivery

7

To prepare for an emergency delivery:

▶ try to get medical help, or

▶ locate an assistant, preferably the father or a woman

▶ assemble the necessary materials, e.g.:

■ clean towels, sheets

■ baby blanket

■ sterile tape or narrow roller bandage to tie off the cord

■ absorbent material to absorb vaginal bleeding after delivery

▶ container for placenta

▶ soap, water and towels to wash your hands

▶ gloves, sterile, if possible

Some of these items such as diapers, receiving blanket, may be found in the materials that the mother has packed for the hospital.

8

Which of the following listed items and people, would be most useful in an emergency childbirth situation?

Check ☑ the correct answers.

☐ A. Adhesive bandages   ☐ F. People passing by

☐ B. Clean cloths   ☐ G. A plastic bag

☐ C. Sanitary pads   ☐ H. Clean wraps for the baby

☐ D. Clean sheeting   ☐ I. Strong thick cord

☐ E. A close friend or relative

9

To **prepare the mother** for delivery:

▶ provide reassurance, comfort and **privacy**

▶ during labour, let the mother find the position of most comfort, usually on the left side. (If she wants to lie on her back, place a folded towel under her right hip. This will help shift the baby off the mother's main blood vessels.)

▶ when birth is imminent, place the mother on her back with knees bent and head supported on a pillow, unless she prefers another position

▶ place clean sheets or towels under her buttocks and between her thighs

▶ cover her with sheets or towels so that you can easily lift the cover to check the progress of labour

10

Mark each of the following statements on how you should prepare the mother for delivery as true **(T)** or false **(F)**.

☐ A. Keep the mother as calm and relaxed as possible.

☐ B. Find a large number of assistants to help speed up the birth.

☐ C. Help the mother to be as comfortable as possible.

☐ D. Place clean materials under and over the mother.

☐ E. Insist that the mother stay on her back during labour and delivery.

A.T B.F C.T D.T E.F

First aid during delivery

11

In preparing for the emergency delivery, keep in mind that **the aims** are to:

▶ **assist** the mother in delivering her baby

▶ **protect** the **mother and baby** during and after delivery until they are handed over to medical help

▶ **send** all parts of the placenta and layers of the amniotic sac to the hospital with the mother

Do not interfere with the natural birth process, particularly during the last stage of labour.

The baby's head will usually be born first. If the head comes out too quickly, the baby may be harmed and the mother injured.

To prevent injury to the baby:

▶ tell the mother **to control** her **pushing**. Ask her to try panting—that helps to prevent the urge to bear down

▶ use **very gentle control** with the palm of your hand on the baby's head to slow its delivery

▶ once the head is delivered, ask the mother to **stop pushing**

▶ check the neck area for the umbilical cord; if not present ask the mother to continue pushing

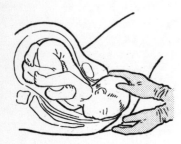 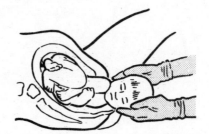 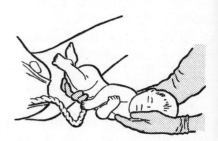

As the baby is being delivered, carefully support the head and body. Remember, the baby is wet and slippery.

12

Check ☑ the correct statements regarding first aid during the birth of a baby.

☐ A. Delivery is a natural process accomplished by the mother's body.

☐ B. Your role, as a first aider, is to ensure the safety of the mother and the infant.

☐ C. Once the top of the head is visible, tell the mother to press down harder.

☐ D. Place both hands around the baby's head and pull it out of the birth canal.

☐ E. Gently and securely hold the newborn when it is emerging from the birth canal.

13

A baby may be born with the **umbilical cord** around his neck.

▶ **Check** the infant's neck

Should the umbilical cord be wrapped around the neck:

▶ ask the mother **to stop pushing**

▶ **slide** your fingers under the cord and loosen it gently

There should be enough slack to allow you to:

▶ **slip** the cord over the baby's head or the upper shoulder

Do not pull or exert force on the cord.

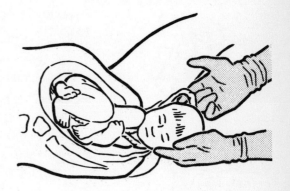

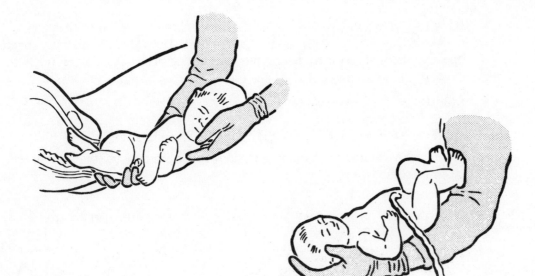

14

Which of the following procedures should you do if a baby is born with the umbilical cord around his neck?

Check ☑ the correct answers.

- ☐ A. Cut the cord immediately.
- ☐ B. Loosen the cord gently.
- ☐ C. Pull the baby's head through the loop of the cord.
- ☐ D. Ease the cord away from the baby's neck.
- ☐ E. Support the baby's head during the procedure.
- ☐ F. Wait for medical help to remove the cord.

B D E

Care of the new-born baby

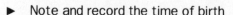

15

Newborns are covered with a whitish, **slippery coating** that makes them difficult to hold. Handle the baby **firmly**, **carefully** and **gently** and keep her at **birth canal level** until the umbilical cord stops pulsating.

▶ Note and record the time of birth

▶ Keep the baby on her side with the head lower than the body to clear fluids from the airway

▶ Wipe the baby's face to clear mucus from the nose and mouth

The baby will probably breathe and cry almost immediately.

▶ If the baby does not breathe on her own, stimulate the baby by rubbing the back gently or by slapping the soles of the feet . **Do not** hang the baby upside down by her heels and slap her on the back or buttocks

▶ Start mouth-to-mouth-and-nose AR if there is no response

▶ Start CPR if there is no pulse

When the baby is breathing and crying, and the cord stops pulsating:

▶ dry the baby with a towel, but do **not remove** the slippery coating; it will be absorbed

▶ keep the baby warm

▶ place the baby on her side on the mother's abdomen, with head lowered

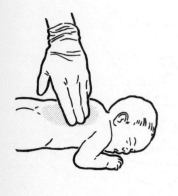

▶ continue to watch baby's breathing and wait for the placenta to be delivered

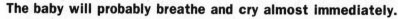

16

Choose ☑ the procedures you should take when caring for a new-born baby.

☐ A. Use both hands and hold the baby with extreme care.

☐ B. Keep the newborn at the level of the vagina and clean her mouth and nose immediately after delivery.

☐ C. To ensure a clear airway, hold the baby upside down by the ankles.

☐ D. Slap the baby between the shoulder blades if she is not breathing.

☐ E. When the baby cries, dry and wrap her in a warm towel.

☐ F. When you can no longer feel a pulse in the cord, lay the baby sideways with the head lowered on the mother's stomach.

A B E F

Care of the umbilical cord and placenta

17

The **umbilical cord** connects the baby to the placenta. The **placenta** will usually be delivered within 20 minutes following the baby's birth.

▶ **Never attempt to force delivery of the placenta by pulling on the cord**

To assist:

▶ gently massage the mother's lower abdomen to stimulate contractions

▶ catch the placenta in a clean towel, bag or basin

▶ ensure that all parts of the placenta are saved

▶ keep the placenta at the same level as the newborn

▶ place the placenta in a clean towel and wrap it with the infant for transportation to the hospital

If medical help is close by and there is no obvious bleeding from the placenta, do not tie or cut the umbilical cord!

If there is **obvious bleeding** from the placenta, **act quickly!**

▶ **Place 2 ties** 7.5 cm (3 inches) apart, 15 to 30 cm (6 to 12 inches) from the baby's navel, using a clean tape or heavy string. **Take care not to cut the cord with the tie!**

▶ Keep the placenta at the same level as the newborn

▶ Transport as soon as possible to the hospital

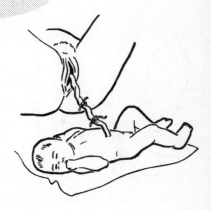

18

Mark each of the following statements as true **(T)** or false **(F)**.

☐ A. Once the baby has been born, tug on the umbilical cord to speed up delivery of the placenta.

☐ B. After delivery of the placenta, you should immediately cut the umbilical cord with sterile scissors.

☐ C. You should keep all pieces of the placenta for examination by medical personnel.

☐ D. Once the placenta is delivered, you should cover it and keep it away from the baby.

☐ E. If there is no bleeding from the placenta, you should leave the umbilical cord alone.

A. F B. F C. T D. F E. T

Care of the mother after delivery

19

To care for the mother after delivery of the placenta:

▶ examine the skin between the anus and vagina for tears (injury) and apply pressure to the wounds

▶ remove soiled sheet

▶ place sanitary pads over the vagina to absorb bleeding

▶ massage the lower abdomen every 5–10 minutes to help the uterus contract and control bleeding

▶ let the baby suck from her mother's breasts; this will help to keep the uterus contracted

▶ position the mother comfortably and keep her warm

▶ give emotional support and arrange for transportation as soon as possible

Should the bleeding from the vagina be excessive:

▶ continue massaging the lower abdomen every 5–10 minutes

▶ place the mother into the shock position

▶ keep the mother and the baby warm

▶ transport immediately to the closest medical facility

Do not use a pillow if bleeding is severe

20

Check ☑ the actions you should take to care for the mother after delivery.

☐ A. Control bleeding from wounds that may have resulted from the delivery.

☐ B. Allow the mother to feed her baby.

☐ C. Place several sterile napkins into the vaginal space.

☐ D. To help stop bleeding, gently but firmly massage the area over the uterus from time to time.

☐ E. Position the mother with the legs and feet raised about 30 cm (12 inches).

☐ F. Keep mother and baby cool.

A B D E

Miscarriage

. . . .

21

Miscarriage, also called **spontaneous abortion,** is the natural loss of the fetus before it is capable of survival outside the uterus (before the twentieth week of pregnancy).

Miscarriage can be classified into 3 types

Threatened miscarriage   Inevitable miscarriage   Complete miscarriage

Signs and symptoms

The woman, knowing or suspecting that she is pregnant, may complain of:

▶ vaginal bleeding, often heavy

▶ cramp-like pains in the lower abdomen

▶ backache

▶ passage of tissue

Emergency Care

▶ Give first aid for shock

▶ Place casualty into the shock position or on her left side

▶ Transport to the nearest medical facility as soon as possible

▶ Take any passed tissue or evidence of blood loss (bloody sheets, towels, underwear) to the hospital for the examining doctor

▶ Provide emotional support

Do not use a pillow if bleeding is severe

Keep the woman warm

. . . .

22

What first aid should you give to a woman in her early stages of pregnancy who shows signs of having lost her baby and is upset and crying?

Check ☑ the correct answers.

▢ A. Provide sanitary pads to absorb the bleeding.

▢ B. Lay the woman down with legs and feet raised about 30 cm (12 inches).

▢ C. Have her rest at home until bleeding stops, then call for medical help.

▢ D. Dispose of any matter that has been passed with the blood.

▢ E. Show sympathy and understanding for the woman's feelings.

A B E

Objectives

. . . .

Upon completion of this activity book exercise, in an emergency situation, you will be able to:

▶ recognize when childbirth is imminent

▶ make preparations for an emergency delivery

▶ provide first aid in an emergency delivery

▶ recognize the signs of a miscarriage

▶ provide first aid for a miscarriage

For further information on emergency childbirth and miscarriage, please refer to: *First on the Scene*, the St. John Ambulance first aid and CPR manual, chapter 13, available through your instructor or any major bookstore in your area.

Emergency scene management—Responsive casualty

An adult casualty has fallen and hit her head, and is lying face up. The casualty can speak clearly and open her eyes when spoken to. Two bystanders are present who witnessed the incident.

Activity	Performance Guidelines

Activity

SCENE SURVEY

- take charge of the situation

- call out for help
- assess hazards at the scene
- determine the number of casualties, what happened, and the mechanism of injury

- identify yourself and offer to help
- send for medical help

- assess responsiveness

PRIMARY SURVEY (ABCs)

- airway

- breathing

- circulation

SECONDARY SURVEY

ONGOING CASUALTY CARE

- monitor casualty's condition
- record the events

- report on what happened

Performance Guidelines

Approach from within the casualty's line of sight. Tell the casualty not to move

Ask bystanders to standby

Make the area safe. To protect yourself, put on latex or vinyl gloves

Question the casualty to determine what happened and the mechanism of injury [*Head/spinal injuries are suspected*]

Identify yourself and ask for consent

Give the following information: what happened, location, and the condition of the casualty

Provide support for the casualty's head and neck since head/spinal injuries are suspected—ask, "Are you OK?" [*A conscious casualty **is** responsive*]

A Ask the casualty, "Where are you hurt?" [*The casualty can speak clearly therefore has a clear airway*]

Instruct a bystander to steady and support the casualty's head and neck

B Check for effectiveness of breathing. Ask, "How is your breathing?" [*The casualty moans.*] Place a hand on the casualty's chest and count the number of breaths per minute

C Check skin condition and temperature [*skin is pale, warm and dry*] Check for hidden, severe, external bleeding and signs of internal bleeding with the rapid body survey [*Casualty has no apparent bleeding or deformities*]

[*Secondary survey is not required as medical help will arrive soon*]

Continue support for the head and neck and do not move the casualty

Reassure the casualty and loosen tight clothing at the neck, chest and waist. Cover the casualty. Do not give anything by mouth

Recheck ABCs often

Take notes of the casualty's condition and any changes that may occur—protect the casualty's belongings

Tell medical attendants what happened, the casualty's condition and what first aid was given [*Casualty remains conscious*]

Emergency scene management—Unresponsive casualty

An unconscious adult casualty is lying face up. The first aider witnessed the casualty's collapse. There is a bystander nearby.

Activity

Performance Guidelines

SCENE SURVEY

- take charge of the situation

- call out for help and assess hazards at the scene

- determine the number of casualties, what happened, and the mechanism of injury

- identify yourself and offer to help

- assess responsiveness

- send for medical help

PRIMARY SURVEY (ABCs)

- airway

- breathing

- circulation

Approach from within the casualty's line of sight

Ask bystanders to standby. Make the area safe. To protect yourself, put on latex or vinyl gloves

Since you witnessed the incident, you know what happened and the mechanism of injury *[You do not suspect head or spinal injuries]*

Identify yourself and ask for consent. If the casualty doesn't respond, you have implied consent

Ask, "Are you O.K.?" and gently tap the casualty's shoulders *[Casualty does not respond]*

Give the following information: what happened, location, and that the casualty is unresponsive

A   Open the airway using the head-tilt, chin-lift

B   Look, listen and feel for 3-5 seconds to check for breathing *[Casualty is breathing]*

Assess the quality and the rate of breathing by placing a hand on the casualty's chest

[Breathing is quiet and occurs without effort and with an even, steady rhythm]

C   Check skin condition and temperature *[Skin is pale, warm and dry]*
Check for hidden, severe, external bleeding and signs of internal bleeding using the rapid body survey *[Casualty has no apparent bleeding or deformities]*

SECONDARY SURVEY

ONGOING CASUALTY CARE

- monitor casualty's condition

- record the events

- report on what happened

[Secondary survey is not required as medical help will arrive soon]

Reassure the casualty and loosen tight clothing at the neck, chest and waist.
If possible, place a blanket underneath the casualty before turning. Place the casualty into the **recovery position**. Cover the casualty, do not give anything by mouth. Protect the belongings

Reassess ABCs

Take notes of the casualty's condition and any changes that may occur

Tell medical attendants what happened. *[Casualty remains unconscious]*

Recovery position—Walk around method

An unconscious adult casualty is lying face up with no apparent injuries. There is a bystander. The scene survey and primary survey have been performed.

Activity

SCENE SURVEY

- take charge of the situation
- call out for help
- assess hazards at the scene
- determine the number of casualties, what happened, and the mechanism of injury
- identify yourself and offer to help
- assess responsiveness
- send for medical help

PRIMARY SURVEY (ABCs)

- airway
- breathing
- circulation

SECONDARY SURVEY

ONGOING CASUALTY CARE

- give first aid for shock
- monitor casualty's condition
- record the events
- report on what happened

Performance Guidelines

You have taken charge

You have called out for help and a bystander responded

You have made the area safe

You have questioned the bystander *(You do not suspect head/spinal injuries)*

You have identified yourself and asked for consent

You have assessed responsiveness *[The casualty is unresponsive]*

A bystander has been sent to call medical help

A   [The casualty has an open airway]

B   [The casualty is breathing effectively]

C   [The casualty is not bleeding but is in shock]

[Secondary survey is not required as medical help will arrive soon]

Reassure. Loosen tight clothing. Place into the recovery position. Cover. Do not give anything by mouth

Check ABCs often

Take notes. Protect belongings

Tell medical attendants the casualty's condition and the first aid given
(Casualty remains unconscious)

Artificial respiration—Adult

An adult casualty is lying face down. The first aider witnessed the incident. A bystander is present.

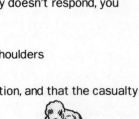

Activity	**Performance Guidelines**
SCENE SURVEY	
• take charge of the situation	Approach from within the casualty's line of sight
• call out for help and assess hazards	Ask the bystander to standby . Make the area safe. To protect yourself, put on latex or vinyl gloves
• determine the number of casualties, what happened, and the mechanism of injury	Since you witnessed the incident, you know what happened and the mechanism of injury *[You do not suspect head or spinal injuries]*
• identify yourself and offer to help	Identify yourself and ask for consent. If the casualty doesn't respond, you have implied consent
• assess responsiveness	Ask, "Are you O.K.?" and gently tap the casualty's shoulders *[Casualty does not respond]*
• send for medical help	Give the following information: what happened, location, and that the casualty is unresponsive

PRIMARY SURVEY (ABCs)	Turn the casualty onto her back
• airway	A Open the airway using the head-tilt chin-lift
• breathing	B Look, listen and feel for 3-5 seconds to check for breathing *[Casualty is not breathing]* Give two slow breaths (1.5-2 seconds each) using enough air to make the chest rise Check to see if the chest rises and falls with each breath *[The chest rises and falls]*
• circulation	C Use two fingers and check for a carotid pulse for 5-10 seconds *[There is a pulse]*
	Continue ventilations. One slow breath every five seconds for about one minute
	Maintain head tilt and recheck pulse and breathing for 5 seconds after one minute (and every few minutes thereafter)
Complete the primary survey check effectiveness of breathing	*(The casualty is now breathing]* Check the rate, rhythm and quality of breathing *[Breathing is effective)*
check circulation	Check for shock. A rapid body survey *is not required as other injuries are not suspected.* [Casualty is in shock]
SECONDARY SURVEY	*[Secondary survey is not required as medical help will arrive soon)*
ONGOING CASUALTY CARE	
• give first aid for shock	Reassure the casualty and loosen tight clothing at the neck, chest and waist. Place the casualty into the **recovery position**. Cover the casualty, do not give anything by mouth. Protect belongings
• monitor casualty's condition and record the events	Reassess ABCs. Take notes of the casualty's condition and any changes that may occur
• report on what happened	Present an oral report to medical attendants

Artificial respiration using jaw-thrust without head-tilt

A casualty has fallen down stairs and is lying face up, at the bottom of a staircase. A bystander is present.

Activity	**Performance Guidelines**

SCENE SURVEY

- take charge of the situation

Approach from within the casualty's line of sight. Tell the casualty not to move

- call out for help and assess hazards at the scene

Ask the bystander to stand by. Make the area safe. To protect yourself, put on latex or vinyl gloves

- determine the number of casualties, what happened, and the mechanism of injury

Question the bystander to determine what happened and the mechanism of injury *[Head/spinal injuries are suspected]*

- identify yourself and offer to help

Identify yourself and ask for consent. If the casualty doesn't respond, you have implied consent

- assess responsiveness

Provide support for the casualty's head and neck since head/spinal injuries are suspected—ask, "Are you OK?"

- send for medical help

Give the following information: what happened, location, and that the casualty is unresponsive

PRIMARY SURVEY (ABCs)

- airway

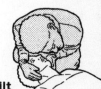

You do not want to move the casualty unnecessarily because of the suspected head/spinal injuries—check for breathing in the position found for 3-5 seconds **before** opening the airway   *[Casualty is not breathing]*

- breathing

A   Open the airway with the **jaw-thrust without head-tilt**

B   Recheck breathing for 3-5 seconds*[Casualty is still not breathing]*
Cover the casualty's mouth with your mouth and seal the nose with your cheek. Give two slow breaths using enough air to make the chest rise
Check to see if the chest rises and falls with each breath *[Chest rises and falls]*

- circulation

C   Maintain support for the head and neck while checking for a pulse for 5-10 seconds *[There is a pulse]*

Continue artificial respiration (one breath every five seconds) until the casualty starts breathing, medical help takes over, another first aider takes over, or you are physically exhausted and unable to continue

Recheck pulse and breathing for five seconds after one minute and every few minutes after that

[Secondary survey is not required as medical help will arrive soon]

SECONDARY SURVEY

ONGOING CASUALTY CARE

- give first aid for shock

Continue support for the head and neck—in this situation **do not** put the casualty into recovery position nor raise the feet because of suspected head/spinal injuries— cover the casualty—protect the casualty's belongings

- monitor casualty's condition and record the events

Reassess ABCs. Take notes of the casualty's condition and any changes that may occur

- report on what happened

Present an oral report to medical attendants [Casualty remains unconscious]

Choking–Adult conscious becoming unconscious

An adult casualty is grasping at her throat and coughing forcefully. A bystander is present.

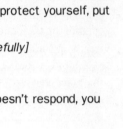

Activity

SCENE SURVEY

- take charge of the situation
- call out for help and assess hazards at the scene
- determine the number of casualties, what happened, and the mechanism of injury
- identify yourself and offer to help

PRIMARY SURVEY (ABCs)

- airway

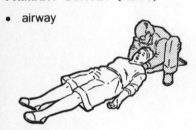

- send for medical help

- breathing

- circulation

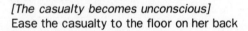

  Complete the primary survey

SECONDARY SURVEY

ONGOING CASUALTY CARE

Performance Guidelines

Approach from within the casualty's line of sight

Ask the bystander to stand by. Make the area safe. To protect yourself, put on latex or vinyl gloves

Ask "Are you choking?" [The casualty is coughing forcefully]

Identify yourself and ask for consent. If the casualty doesn't respond, you have implied consent

A   Do not intervene at this time—encourage coughing
Watch for signs of complete obstruction

[The casualty now cannot cough, breathe or speak] When coughing stops, ask "Can you cough?" Stand behind the casualty and landmark—give inward and upward abdominal thrusts until the airway is cleared or the casualty becomes unconscious

[The casualty becomes unconscious]
Ease the casualty to the floor on her back

Give the following information: what happened, location, and that the casualty is choking and unconscious

Open mouth using the tongue-jaw lift — use the index finger to finger weep the mouth [Nothing is dislodged]

Tild the head using the head-tilt chin-lift, seal the mouth and nose and try to ventilate [Chest does not rise]

Reposition the head, check the seals and try to ventilate again [Chest still does not rise]

Straddle the casualty's legs, landmark and give up to five inward/upward abdominal thrusts—repeat finger sweeps, attempts to ventilate and abdominal thrusts until the airway is cleared, medical help takes over or you cannot continue any longer
[The object is seen and removed]

B   Give 1 slow breath checking that the chest rises and falls [Chest rises and falls.] Give a second breath, watching the chest rise and fall

C   Check for a carotid pulse and breathing for 5-10 seconds [The casualty has a pulse and is breathing, but remains unconscious] Assess the quality and rate of breathing by placing a hand on the casualty's chest. Check circulation (skin temperature and condition). [Breathing is effective, skin is cold and clammy]

[Secondary survey is not required as medical help will arrive soon]

Give first aid for shock, monitor casualty's condition. Continue to check ABCs until medical help takes over. Record the events along with any changes that may occur and report to medical attendants when they arrive

Choking—Adult (pregnant or obese)

A woman in an advanced stage of pregnancy appears to be choking and she cannot cough, breathe or speak. A bystander is present.

Activity

Performance Guidelines

SCENE SURVEY

- take charge of the situation

- call out for help and assess hazards at the scene

- determine the number of casualties, what happened, and the mechanism of injury

- identify yourself and offer to help

Approach from within the casualty's line of sight

Ask the bystander to stand by. Make the area safe. To protect yourself, put on latex or vinyl gloves

Ask "Are you choking?" [The casualty cannot cough, breathe or speak]

You have identified yourself and asked for consent. If the casuatly doesn't respond, you have implied consent

PRIMARY SURVEY (ABCs)

- airway

A   Identify the degree of obstruction

Ask "Can you cough?" Stand behind the casualty and landmark—give inward **chest** thrusts until the airway is cleared or the casualty becomes unconscious

[The casualty becomes unconscious]
Ease the casualty to the floor on her back. Place a wedge under her right hip, if readily available

- send for medical help

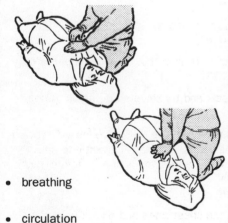

Give the following information: what happened, location, the number of casualties and that the casualty is choking, and unconscious

Open mouth using the tongue-jaw lift — finger-sweep the mouth [Nothing is dislodged]

Tilt the head using the head-tilt chin-lift, seal the mouth and nose, and try to ventilate [Chest does not rise]

Reposition the head, check the seals and try to ventilate again [Chest still does not rise]

Kneel at the casualty's side and landmark and give up to five distinct **chest** thrusts—repeat finger sweeps, attempts to ventilate and chest thrusts until the airway is cleared, medical help takes over or you cannot continue any longer [The object is seen and removed]

- breathing

B   Give 1 slow breath checking that the chest rises and falls. [Chest rises and falls] Give a second breath, watching the chest rise and fall

- circulation

  Complete the primary survey

C   Check for a carotid pulse and breathing for 5-10 seconds. [The casualty has a pulse and is breathing, but remains unconscious] Assess the quality and rate of breathing by placing a hand on the casualty's chest. Check circulation (skin temperature and condition) [Breathing is effective, skin is cold and clammy]

SECONDARY SURVEY

[Secondary survey is not required as medical help will arrive soon]

ONGOING CASUALTY CARE

Give first aid for shock, monitor casuatly's condition. Continue to check ABCs until medical help takes over. Record the events, with any changes that may occur and report to medical attendants when they arrive

One rescuer CPR–Adult

An adult casualty is lying face up. There are no bystanders. The first aider witnessed the incident. There is a telephone nearby.

Activity

Performance Guidelines

SCENE SURVEY

- take charge of the situation

  Approach from within the casualty's line of sight

- call out for help and assess hazards at the scene

  Make the area safe. To protect yourself, put on latex or vinyl gloves

- determine the number of casualties, what happened, and the mechanism of injury

  You witnessed the collapse and you do not suspect head or spinal injuries

- identify yourself and offer to help

  Identify yourself and ask for consent. If the casualty doesn't respond, you have implied consent

- assess responsiveness

  Ask, "Are you O.K.?" and gently tap the casualty's shoulders *[Casualty does not respond]*

- send/call for medical help

  Give the following information: what happened, location, and that the casualty is unresponsive

PRIMARY SURVEY (ABCs)

- airway
- breathing

  A Open the airway using the head-tilt, chin-lift

  B Look, listen and feel for 3-5 seconds to check for breathing *[Casualty is not breathing]* Give two slow breaths (1.5-2 seconds each) watchingthe chest to make sure it rises and falls *[The chest rises and falls]*

- circulation

  C Use two fingers and check the carotid pulse for 5-10 seconds *[There is no pulse]*

  Locate the bottom edge of the rib cage, and landmark for chest compressions
  Keep arms straight, elbows locked in position and shoulders positioned directly above the heel of the hands so that each compression is straight down on the breastbone

Give cycles of 15 compressions and 2 slow ventilations for about one minute. Use any memory aid to maintain the correct rate of 80-100 compressions per minute, e.g.:

> 1 and 2 and 3 and 4 and 5 and
>
> 1 and 2 and 3 and 4 and 10 and
>
> 1 and 2 and 3 and 4 and 15

Recheck pulse and breathing for 5 seconds, after one minute and every few minutes after that *[There is still no breathing or pulse]*

Continue CPR until the pulse is restored, until medical help takes over, until another first aider trained in CPR takes over or until you are physically exhausted and unable to continue *[The casualty is not breathing and has no pulse]*

SECONDARY SURVEY

ONGOING CASUALTY CARE

In this situation the first aider continues CPR until medical help arrives. The first aider has not progressed from the primary survey before help arrives

Two rescuer CPR–Adult

An adult casualty is lying face up. There is a bystander present.

Activity	Performance Guidelines	
	1st rescuer	**2nd rescuer**
First aiders are positioned on opposite sides of the casualty	Start in the role of ventilator	Start in the role of compressor
SCENE SURVEY		
• start scene survey	Take charge, call out for help, assess hazards, make area safe, determine what happened, identify yourself and offer to help	Assist with scene survey if needed
	Assess responsiveness[*Casualty does not respond*]	Stand by
	Send the bystander for medical help	

PRIMARY SURVEY (ABCs)

- airway
- breathing

1st rescuer	2nd rescuer
Open the airway	
Check for breathing [*Casualty is not breathing*] Give 2 slow ventilations. [*The chest rises and falls with each ventilation*]	

- circulation

1st rescuer	2nd rescuer
Check carotid pulse for 5-10 seconds [*There is no pulse*]	Landmark for correct hand position.

Perform cycles of 5 compressions and 1 ventilation for about **one minute** (ten cycles)

1st rescuer	2nd rescuer
Give one slow ventilation after each set of 5 compressions and then monitor compressions	**Give 5 compressions**—Use a memory aid to achieve the correct rate of 80-100 compressions per minute, e.g.: 1 and 2 and 3 and 5 and pause, keeping hands in position to allow for one slow ventilation from the ventilator
After one minute, say "Stop compressions" Complete the cycle with one ventilation before checking for a pulse and breathing [*There is still no pulse*].	**Pause,** keeping hands in position
Say "no pulse, resume compressions"	Continue with cycles of 5 compressions

Continue CPR for a few minutes and then proceed with a **switch-over**

1st rescuer	2nd rescuer
Check for pulse and breathing every few minutes, after the ventilation cycle.	After a set of 5 compressions, say "switch"
Give 1 slow ventilation then move to the chest and landmark to take new role as compressor	**Move into position beside the head and prepare to check for pulse and breathing** to take new role as ventilator

SEC.SURVEY/ONGOING CARE
The first aiders continue CPR until medical help takes over

1st rescuer	2nd rescuer
Resume compressions	**Confirm no pulse and say, "no pulse,** resume compressions"

Artificial respiration—Child

A child casualty is lying face down. The first aider witnessed the incident. A guardian is present.

Activity	Performance Guidelines
SCENE SURVEY	
• take charge of the situation	Approach from within the casualty's line of sight
• call out for help and assess hazards	Ask the parent or guardian to standby. Make the area safe. To protect yourself, put on latex or vinyl gloves
• determine the number of casualties, what happened, and the mechanism of injury	Question the guardian to determine what happened and the mechanism of injury *[Head/spinal injuries are not suspected]*
• identify yourself and offer to help	Identify yourself and ask for consent from the guardian
• assess responsiveness	Ask, "Are you O.K.?" and gently tap the child's shoulders *[Child does not respond]*
• send for medical help	Give the following information: what happened, location, and that the child is unresponsive
PRIMARY SURVEY (ABCs)	Turn the child onto his back
• airway	A Open the airway using the head-tilt chin-lift
• breathing	B Look, listen and feel for 3-5 seconds to check for breathing. *[Casualty is not breathing]*. Give two slow breaths (1 to 1.5 seconds each) using just enough air to make the chest rise. Check to see if the chest rises and falls with each breath. *[The chest rises and falls]*
• circulation	C Use two fingers and check the carotid pulse for 5-10 seconds *[There is a pulse]*
	Continue ventilations. One slow breath every five seconds for about one minute
Complete the primary survey	Maintain head tilt and recheck pulse and breathing for 5 seconds after one minute (and every few minutes thereafter)
check breathing	*(The child is now breathing.]* Check the rate, rhythm and quality of breathing *[Breathing is effective)*
check circulation	Check for shock (skin condition and temperature) and do a rapid body survey *[Casualty is in shock but is not bleeding]*
SECONDARY SURVEY	*[Secondary survey is not required as medical help will arrive soon)*
ONGOING CASUALTY CARE	Place the child into the recovery position. Cover, and loosen clothing. Do not give anything by mouth
• give first aid for shock	
• monitor casualty's condition and record the events	Reassess ABCs. Take notes of the child's condition and any changes that may occur
• report on what happened	Present an oral report to medical attendants

Choking–Child conscious becoming unconscious

A child is grasping at his throat and coughing forcefully. A parent or guardian is present.

Activity

SCENE SURVEY

- take charge of the situation
- call out for help and assess hazards at the scene
- determine the number of casualties, what happened, and the mechanism of injury
- identify yourself and offer to help

PRIMARY SURVEY (ABCs)

- airway

- send for medical help

- breathing

- circulation
  Complete primary survey

SECONDARY SURVEY

ONGOING CASUALTY CARE

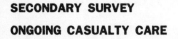

Performance Guidelines

Approach from within the casualty's line of sight

Ask the guardian to stand by. Make the area safe. To protect yourself, put on latex or vinyl gloves

Ask "Are you choking?" [The casualty is coughing forcefully]

Identify yourself and ask for consent from the parent or guardian

A   Do not intervene at this time—encourage coughing
Watch for signs of complete obstruction

[The child now cannot cough, breathe or speak]
When coughing stops, ask "Can you cough?"
Stand or kneel behind the child and landmark—give inward and upward abdominal thrusts until the airway is cleared or the child becomes unconscious

[The child becomes unconscious]
Ease the child to the floor on his back

Give the following information: what happened, location, number of casualties and that the child is choking and unconscious

Open mouth using the tongue-jaw lift —visually check for any foreign objects in the mouth and finger sweep **only** if you see something [Nothing is dislodged]

Tilt the head using the head-tilt chin-lift, seal the mouth and nose and try to ventilate [Chest does not rise]

Reposition the head, check the seals and try to ventilate again [Chest still does not rise]

Straddle the child's legs, landmark and give up to five inward/upward abdominal thrusts—repeat foreign body checks, attempts to ventilate and abdominal thrusts until the airway is cleared, medical help takes over or you cannot continue any longer [The object is seen and removed]

B   Give 1 slow breath (1-1.5 seconds) checking that the chest rises and falls [Chest rises and falls] Give a second breath, watching the chest rise and fall

C   Check for a carotid pulse and breathing for 5-10 seconds [The child has a pulse, and is breathing but remains unconscious] Assess the quality and rate of breathing by placing a hand on the child's chest. Check circulation (skin temperature and condition) [Breathing is effective, skin is cold and clammy]

[Secondary survey is not required as medical help will arrive soon]

Turn into the recovery position and give first aid for shock. Continue to check ABCs until medical help takes over. Record the events along with any changes that may occur and report to medical attendants when they arrive

One rescuer CPR–Child

An unconscious child casualty is lying face up. A parent or guardian who witnessed the incident is present.

Activity

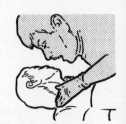

Performance Guidelines

SCENE SURVEY

- take charge of the situation

- call out for help and assess hazards at the scene

Approach from within the casualty's line of sight

Make the area safe. To protect yourself, put on latex or vinyl gloves

- determine the number of casualties, what happened, and the mechanism of injury

Question the parent or guardian to determine what happened and the mechanism of injury. *[Head/spinal injuries are not suspected]*

- identify yourself and offer to help

Identify yourself and ask for consent from the parent or guardian

- assess responsiveness

Ask, "Are you O.K.?" and gently tap the child's shoulders *[Child does not respond]*

- send for medical help

Give the following information: what happened, location, and that the child is unresponsive

PRIMARY SURVEY (ABCs)

- airway

- breathing

A   Open the airway using the head-tilt, chin-lift

B   Look, listen and feel for 3-5 seconds to check for breathing. *[Child is not breathing]*. Give two slow breaths (1 to 1.5 seconds each) watching the chest to make sure it rises and falls *[The chest rises and falls]*

- circulation

C   Check for a carotid pulse for 5-10 seconds *[There is no pulse]*

Locate the bottom edge of the rib cage, and landmark to find the lower part of the breastbone. Give 5 chest compressions with the heel of one hand. Keep arm straight, elbow locked in position and shoulders positioned directly above the heel of the hands so that each compression is straight down on the breastbone. Keep the airway open with the other hand.

Give cycles of 5 compressions and 1 slow ventilation for about one minute. Use any memory aid to maintain the correct rate of 100 compressions per minute, e.g.:

1, 2, 3, 4, 5

Recheck pulse and breathing for 5 seconds, after one minute and every few minutes after that *[There is still no breathing or pulse]*

Continue CPR until the pulse is restored, until medical help takes over, until another first aider trained in CPR takes over or until you are physically exhausted and unable to continue *[The child is not breathing and has no pulse]*

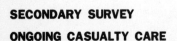

SECONDARY SURVEY
ONGOING CASUALTY CARE

In this situation the first aider continues CPR until medical help arrives. The first aider has not progressed from the primary survey before help arrives

Artificial respiration—Infant

An infant casualty is lying face up. A parent or guardian who witnessed the incident is present.

Activity	**Performance Guidelines**

SCENE SURVEY

- take charge of the situation

Approach from within the casuatly's line of sight

- call out for help and assess hazards at the scene

Make the area safe. To protect yourself, put on latex or vinyl gloves

- determine the number of casualties, what happened, and the mechanism of injury

Question the parent or guardian to determine what happened and the mechanism of injury. [Head/spinal injuries are not suspected]

- identify yourself and offer to help

Identify yourself and ask for consent from the parent or guardian

- assess responsiveness

Gently tap the bottom of the infant's feet [Infant does not respond]

- send for medical help

Give the following information: what happened, location, and that the infant is unresponsive

PRIMARY SURVEY (ABCs)

- airway
- breathing

A   Open the airway using the head-tilt chin-lift

B   Look, listen and feel for 3-5 seconds to check for breathing [Infant is not breathing] Make a good seal over the infant's mouth and nose. Give two slow, breaths using just enough air to make the chest rise. Check to see if the chest rises and falls with each breath.
[The chest rises and falls]

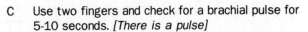

- circulation

C   Use two fingers and check for a brachial pulse for 5-10 seconds. [There is a pulse]

Continue ventilations

Give one slow breath every three seconds for about one minute

Recheck pulse and breathing after one minute (and every few minutes after)

Maintain head tilt. Recheck pulse and breathing for 5 seconds

Continue ventilations until the breathing is restored, until medical help takes over, until another first aider takes over or until you are physically exhausted and unable to continue
[The infant is not breathing, but has a pulse]

SECONDARY SURVEY

ONGOING CASUALTY CARE

In this situation the first aider continues AR until medical help arrives. The first aider has not progressed from the primary survey before help arrives

Choking–Infant conscious becoming unconscious

An infant appears to be struggling and coughing forcefully. A parent or guardian who witnessed the incident is present.

Activity

Performance Guidelines

SCENE SURVEY

- take charge of the situation

Approach from within the casualty's line of sight

- call out for help and assess hazards at the scene

To protect yourself, put on latex or vinyl gloves

- determine the number of casualties, what happened, and the mechanism of injury

Question the parent or guardian to determine what happened and the mechanism of injury. *[Head/spinal injuries are not suspected]*

- identify yourself and offer to help

Identify yourself and ask for consent from the parent or guardian

PRIMARY SURVEY (ABCs)

- airway

A   Identify the degree of obstruction

[The infant is red in the face and gagging].
Position the infant face down with the head lower than the trunk. Give 5 back blows between the shoulder blades then turn the infant. Give 5 chest thrusts with two fingers one finger's width below the nipple line

Repeat back blows and chest thrusts until the obstruction is removed or the infant becomes unconscious
[The infant becomes unconscious]

- send for medical help

Give the following information: what happened, location, and that the infant is unresponsive

Open mouth using the tongue-jaw lift —visually check for any foreign objects in the mouth and finger sweep **only** if you see something.
Tilt the head using the head-tilt chin-lift, seal over the mouth and nose and try to ventilate. *[Chest does not rise]*. Reposition the head, check the seals and try to ventilate again. *[Chest still does not rise]*
Repeat back blows and chest thrusts, foreign body checks, and attempts to ventilate, until the airway is cleared, medical help takes over or you cannot continue. *[The object is seen and removed]*

- breathing

B   Give 1 slow breath (1-1.5 seconds each) checking that the chest rises and falls. *[Chest rises and falls]*. Give a second breath, watching the chest rise and fall. Check for breathing for 3-5 seconds *[The infant is breathing]*.

- circulation

Complete the primary survey

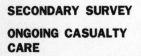

C   Check for a brachial pulse and breathing for 5-10 seconds *[The infant has a pulse and is breathing, but remains unconscious]*

Assess the quality and rate of breathing by placing a hand on the infant's chest. Check circulation (skin temperature and condition) *[Breathing is effective. Skin is cold and clammy]*

SECONDARY SURVEY

ONGOING CASUALTY CARE

[Secondary survey is not required as medical help will arrive soon]

Give first aid for shock, monitor the infant's condition. Continue to check ABCs until medical help takes over. Record the events along with any changes that may occur and report to medical attendants when they arrive

Choking–Infant found unconscious

An unconscious infant is lying face up. A parent or guardian who witnessed the incident is present.

Activity

SCENE SURVEY

- take charge of the situation

- call out for help and assess hazards at the scene

- determine the number of casualties, what happened, and the mechanism of injury

- identify yourself and offer to help

- assess responsiveness

- send for medical help

PRIMARY SURVEY (ABCs)

- airway

- breathing

- circulation

Complete the primary survey

SECONDARY SURVEY

ONGOING CASUALTY CARE

- give first aid for shock

- monitor casualty's condition and record the events

- report on what happened

Performance Guidelines

Approach from within the casualty's line of sight

To protect yourself put on latex or vinyl gloves

Question the parent or guardian to determine what happened and the mechanism of injury. *[Head/spinal injuries are not suspected]*

Identify yourself and ask for consent from the parent or guardian

Gently tap the bottom of the infant's feet *[The infant does not respond]*

Give the following information: what happened, location, and that the infant is unresponsive

A   Open the airway using the head-tilt chin-lift

B   Look, listen and feel for 3-5 seconds to check for breathing *[The infant is not breathing].* Make a good seal over the infant's mouth and nose. Give one slow breath (1-1.5 seconds) using just enough air to make the chest rise. *[The chest does not rise].* Reposition the head, check the seal and try to ventilate again. *[The chest still does not rise]*

Position the infant face down with the head lower than the trunk. Give 5 back blows followed by 5 chest thrusts
Open mouth using the tongue-jaw lift- visually check for any foreign objects in the mouth and finger sweep **only** if you see something. Repeat back blows and chest thrusts, foreign body checks, and attempts to ventilate, until the airway is cleared, medical help takes over or you cannot continue. *[The object is seen and removed]*

Give 1 slow breath (1-1.5 seconds each) checking that the chest rises and falls. *[The chest rises and falls].* Give a second breath. *[The chest rises and falls]*

C   Check for a brachial pulse and breathing for 5-10 seconds
    [The infant has a pulse and is breathing, but remains unconscious]

Assess the quality and rate of breathing. Check circulation (skin temperature and condition). *[Breathing is effective, skin is cold and clammy]*

[Secondary survey is not required as medical help will arrive soon]

Cover the infant, loosen tight clothing at the neck, chest and waist. Reassure the infant and parent

Continue to check ABCs. Record the casualty's condition and any changes that may occur

Tell medical attendants what happened, the infant's condition and what first aid was given

One rescuer CPR–Infant

An unconscious infant is lying face up. A parent or guardian who witnessed the incident is present.

Activity

SCENE SURVEY

- take charge of the situation

- call out for help and assess hazards at the scene

- determine the number of casualties, what happened, and the mechanism of injury

- identify yourself and offer to help

- assess responsiveness

- send for medical help

PRIMARY SURVEY (ABCs)

- airway

- breathing

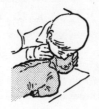

- circulation

SECONDARY SURVEY AND ONGOING CASUALTY CARE

Performance Guidelines

Approach from within the casualty's line of sight

Make the area safe. To protect yourself, put on latex or vinyl gloves

Question the parent or guardian to determine what happened and the mechanism of injury. [Head/spinal injuries are not suspected]

Identify yourself and ask for consent from the parent or guardian

Gently tap the bottom of the infant's feet
[Infant does not respond]

Give the following information: what happened, location, and that the infant is unresponsive

A   Open the airway using the head-tilt chin-lift

B   Look, listen and feel for 3-5 seconds to check for breathing [Infant is not breathing]. Make a good seal over the infant's mouth and nose. Give two slow breaths using just enough air to make the chest rise. Check to see if the chest rises and falls with each breath. [The chest rises and falls]

C   Check for a brachial pulse for 5-10 seconds
[There is no pulse]

Landmark to find the lower part of the breastbone and give 5 compressions with two fingers, one finger width below the nipple line.

Use any memory aid to maintain the correct rate of at least 100 compressions per minute e.g.:
    1, 2, 3, 4, 5

Give cycles of 5 compressions and 1 slow ventilation for about one minute

Recheck pulse and breathing for 5 seconds, after one minute and every few minutes after that. [There is still no breathing or pulse]

Continue CPR until the pulse is restored, until medical help takes over, until another first aider trained in CPR takes over or until you are physically exhausted and unable to continue. [The infant is not breathing and has no pulse]

In this situation the first aider continues CPR until medical help arrives. The first aider has not progressed from the primary survey before help arrives

Answers to the instructor-led exercises

For your reference, the answers to the instructor-led exercises throughout the activity book are given below:

Instructor-led Exercise 4

A1 can
A2 forceful
A3 wheezing
A4 reddish
A5 encourage coughing

B1 cannot
B2 ineffective
B3 high-pitched noises
B4 bluish
B5 first aid

C1 cannot
C2 impossible
C3 no sound; cannot
C4 bluish
C5 first aid

Instructor-led Exercise 8A

1. blood pressure
2. constantly
3a. thick and less elastic
 b. enlarged
4. almost never
5. fatty deposits
6. b
7. coronary artery disease
8. a, b, c, d, f
9. oxygen
10. narrowed
11. blood clot; heart muscle
12. oxygen
13. angina
14. pumping blood
15. sudden death
16. (in any order)
    heart attack
    stroke
    electrical shock
    poisoning
    suffocation
    drowning
17. oxygen
18. blockage; brain
19. stroke

Instructor-led Exercise 8B

Angina/Heart attack

A1 do its work without pain
A2 heart tissue alive
A3 chest
A4 spread
A5 denial; vomiting
A6 scene survey
A7 primary survey
A8 send or go
A10 conscious
A11 medical help takes over

Cardiac arrest

B1 stopped beating; pumping
B3 breathing
B4 pulse
B5 scene survey
B6 responsiveness
B7 send or go
B8 CPR

Stroke/TIA

C1 brain; dies
C2 does not die
C3 changes
C4 pupils
C5 speak
C6 paralyzed
C9 TIA
C10 scene survey
C11 primary survey
C12 send or go
C13 comfortable; loosen
C14 nothing
C15 protect
C16 the recovery position; paralyzed
C17 medical help takes over

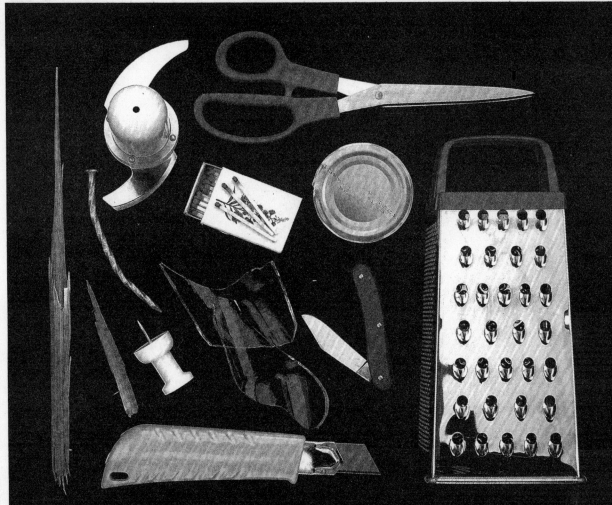

The reasons for buying our Family First Aid Kit are painfully obvious.

Family life is filled with cuts, scrapes and scratches. Some can be serious. The St. John Ambulance Family First Aid Kit provides you with first aid for all types of injuries. It's like a security blanket for the whole family. So order yours today. Being without one could prove to be a pain.

 St. John Ambulance

For details about this or other St. John Ambulance First Aid Kits ask your instructor or contact your local branch.

WHAT NEXT?!

Congratulations!

You have successfully completed a St. John Ambulance First Aid course. What next? Why not put your new skills to use, and become a volunteer member of St. John Ambulance.

Join the Brigade

▶ **serve your community**—provide first aid services at local events, and take part in other programmes such as hospital or school visits.

▶ **learn more first aid, CPR and patient care skills (free of charge)**—ongoing training for Brigade members integrates first aid, CPR and patient care skills along with practical and written assessments.

▶ **develop leadership skills**—take advantage of leadership training and apply it in leadership positions at all levels of the Brigade.

▶ **make new friends**—there are approximately 500 Brigade divisions across the country, made up of over 11,000 people, like yourself, who want to share their time and skills with their communities.

▶ **earn recognition**—your involvement in the Brigade will be appreciated by employers and schools. Your achievements will be recognized through our extensive awards programme.

Become an Instructor

▶ **teach courses to the public**—further your knowledge and techniques through the National Instructor Training and Development Programme, and share your talents through community-based courses.

▶ **earn an honorarium**—expenses incurred by you in implementing courses will be covered by an honorarium.

▶ **help Canadians to help themselves**—with your help, Canadians will learn new skills in the variety of courses offered by St. John Ambulance.

▶ **gain experience speaking in front of a group**—you will have an opportunity to speak to Canadians young and old, and from a variety of cultural backgrounds. Each new group offers new and different challenges.

▶ **develop lasting friendships**—participating as a St. John instructor will have a positive effect on you not only from fellow instructors but also from your students.

Share your skills—join the St. John family.
For more information, contact your local Branch of St. John Ambulance today!

St. John Ambulance